Series / Number 07-068

RASCH MODELS FOR MEASUREMENT

DAVID ANDRICH
Murdoch University

SAGE PUBLICATIONS
The International Professional Publishers
Newbury Park   London   New Delhi

For information address:

SAGE Publications, Inc.
2455 Teller Road
Newbury Park, California 91320
E-mail: order@sagepub.com

SAGE Publications Ltd.
6 Bonhill Street
London EC2A 4PU
United Kingdom

SAGE Publications India Pvt. Ltd.
M-32 Market
Greater Kailash I
New Delhi 110 048 India

International Standard Book Number 0-8039-2741-X

Library of Congress Catalog Card No. L.C. 873-062443

02   03   12   11   10   9   8

When citing a professional paper, please use the proper form. Remember to cite the correct
Sage University Paper series title and include the paper number. One of the two following
formats can be adapted (depending on the style manual used):

(1) IVERSEN, GUDMUND R. and NORPOTH, HELMUT (1976) "Analysis of Variance." Sage University Paper series on Quantitative Applications in the Social Sciences,
07-001. Beverly Hills: Sage Publications.

OR

(2) Iversen, Gudmund R. and Norpoth, Helmut. 1976. *Analysis of Variance.* Sage
University Paper series on Quantitative Applications in the Social Sciences, series no.
07-001. Beverly Hills: Sage Publications.

CONTENTS

Editor's Introduction

Rasch measurement models have been the focus of much recent work in psychology, sociology, and education. Professor Andrich's introduction to Rasch modeling emphasizes general principles rather than the details of the models. He provides explicit connections between Rasch models and the more commonly understood and used procedures for social science measurement. In particular, he relates Rasch models to those models derived from the work of Thurstone and Guttman and those known as Traditional Test Theory. This effort makes the material more accessible and permits the reader to compare and contrast these more familiar approaches and the recent developments in Rasch modeling.

The author attempts to avoid polemics but does so in a way that highlights the controversies engendered in the conflict between the approach of Rasch modeling and other recent work in social science measurement. His intention is to make recent developments sufficiently clear that readers can understand them and make up their own minds. His goal is pedagogy and not mere advocacy.

Professor Andrich restricts his presentation to the case for dichotomous responses to a set of tasks, questions, or items deemed to be conformable. Although the model he discusses has often been labeled *the* Rasch model, it is only the simplest of a class of models that can easily be generalized for other types of data. It can be extended quite comfortably to the case of ordered responses such as Likert-style response formats. Space simply did not permit Professor Andrich to expand his coverage beyond the simple case.

This article presents one extended example, using only six items of a personality inventory. The analysis of this example is presented in conjunction with the development of the model, clarifying the relationship between model and data. In order to elucidate other issues, Professor Andrich uses a data set with a larger number of items and relies on an artificial example. He does so to illustrate how the data are rearranged for estimation and how the parameter estimates fit into the solution equations.

We are pleased to add an introduction to Rasch models to the *Quantitative Applications* series. If the responses of our readers are sufficiently positive, we may add a more advanced monograph that goes beyond dichotomous responses and generalizes *the* Rasch model. Professor Andrich's monograph, taken together with those already published on *Achievement Testing, Test Item Bias, Magnitude Scaling, Unidimensional Scaling, Reliability and Validity Assessment*, and *Multidimensional Scaling*, provides a comprehensive and coherent introduction to the core topics in social science measurement. We believe that researchers in psychology, education, sociology, political science, and marketing, as well as other fields, will find this set of articles invaluable in their attempts to understand and utilize state-of-the-art social science measurement techniques.

—*John L. Sullivan*
Series Coeditor

RASCH MODELS FOR MEASUREMENT

DAVID ANDRICH
Murdoch University

1. MAGNITUDES AND QUANTITIES: DIFFERENCES IN DEGREE

Magnitude or quantity is a common concept in everyday discourse (Ellis, 1966). It is common in physical properties, such as those of height, strength of electric current, or loudness of sound, and with social or psychological phenomena, in which ideas of better or worse, higher or lower, and more or less abound. We can think of people who are better or worse at reading, higher or lower in socioeconomic status, and more or less neurotic.

For scientific work, it is necessary to operationalize magnitudes. This operationalization is generally termed *variable construction*. When a variable has been constructed, magnitudes of the property in entities, which are restricted to persons in this volume, can be measured. While it is the property that is measured, we usually say that a person has been measured. The importance of measures is that arithmetical operations made on them can be interpreted.

Unidimensionality. Every person can be characterized by many properties; however, in constructing a variable we identify individual differences that can be mapped on a single real number line. Such a variable then is unidimensional. More than one variable can be considered simultaneously (Kruskal and Wish, 1978), but in this book we confine ourselves to unidimensional variables.

It is essential to clarify three related points on unidimensionality. First, *unidimensionality is a relative matter*—every human perfor-

AUTHOR'S NOTE: *The help of Irene Dawes, Graham Douglas, Jim Tognolini, Lesley Van Shoubroeck, and Ben Wright, who read through the manuscript, and of Irene Dawes, Graham Douglas, and Alan Lyne, who helped with the data analyses, is very much appreciated, as is the permission of the State Education Department of Western Australia to use the data in the first illustrative example.*

9

mance, action, or belief is complex and involves a multitude of component abilities, interests, and so on. Nevertheless, there are circumstances in which it is considered useful to think of concepts in unidimensional terms, as we will illustrate in the context of an example. Second, a *unidimensional variable is constructed*—it makes a great deal of ingenuity and knowledge of the subject matter to establish a variable that is unidimensional to a level of precision that is of some practical or theoretical use. This point helps us appreciate why constructing variables in both the physical and social sciences is important: *Where relevant*, successful measurement demonstrates a great deal of understanding of the property. Often, devising a measuring instrument is as important in what it teaches about the variable as are the subsequent acts of measurement using the instrument. Third, with unidimensional measurements, *comparisons can be made using their differences*. Such differences are differences in *degree*. Differences that are not differences in degree are said to be differences in *kind*, and both are important.

The observation framework and the frame of reference. Before numbers can be assigned to properties, it is necessary to observe their manifestations. Often, researchers observe such manifestations in naturally occurring situations, and they tend to note the circumstances under which the manifestations are observed. Thus they might observe, say, neurotic behavior. For more detailed study, however, this method may be considered cumbersome, time consuming, and uncontrolled. Therefore, situations are contrived in order to manifest either the property or a proxy for the property. For example, to obtain information about neuroticism, statements about feelings related to neurotic behavior may be presented to persons who are then required to agree or disagree with the statements.

While the contrived situations provide controls, they are removed from natural settings and, therefore, their validity may be reduced. Thus the challenge for the researcher is to create controlled situations that nevertheless are valid for the purpose at hand. The controlled situation, which directs and structures the observations, is referred to here as the *observation framework*. This framework must be rendered as explicit as possible to ensure that intended observations, and not others, are made, to ensure consistency of observations, and to permit replications of the procedure. The observation framework is derived from a *frame of reference* that is specified to circumscribe the application and interpretation of the construct.

Discrete observations. Observations tend to be discrete, even when we think of properties that we conceive of as continuous. Thus we may infer the degree to which persons are neurotic by having them say something about how they feel about themselves. If we wish to formalize what they say, we may present them with some statements and ask them to agree or disagree with the statements. Their responses then are discrete.

Mathematical models. To obtain measurements from discrete observations, it is necessary to transform the observations by a model of one kind or another, and in this volume we are concerned with a particular case of a class of mathematical models called "Rasch models for measurement." They are called Rasch models because of the epistemological case advanced for them by the Danish mathematician Georg Rasch (1901-1980). (See Rasch, 1960/1980, 1961).

While mathematical models can be classified in different ways, one important distinction is between deterministic and statistical models.

Deterministic models. The use of a deterministic model implies an exact prediction of an outcome. For example, from the well-known law f = ma within Newton's theory of gravitation, it is expected that if an object of mass m is submitted to a mechanical force f, then its acceleration a can be calculated (or predicted). It is known, of course, that the prediction will not be perfect, that inevitably there will be some error. However, the error is not incorporated in the model because the values of interest (the f, m, and a) are sufficiently great relative to the errors that the latter are swamped; they need to be considered only informally in the model.

Within the frame of reference, the model attempts to account for all the relevant causes of the outcome, and one task for scientists is to extend the frame of reference. Part of this task is to discover where the model does not apply. Eventually, it may turn out that there are conditions in which a model itself needs to be modified (Kuhn, 1970). We will explore this issue further in the context of an example.

Statistical models. In contrast to the application of a deterministic model, a statistical model is applied when it is not expected (i) that the model accounts for all the relevant causes of the outcome, (ii) that the differences in outcomes in ideal replications can be ignored, or (iii) that the same outcome will result from the same known circumstances. Different known circumstances may produce the same outcome and vice versa. As a result, the outcomes are formalized in terms of probabilities.

Replications. In statistical models, it is necessary to be able to indicate the possible outcomes; then the probability of each outcome can be viewed as the proportion of times in an infinite number of *replications* that the outcome would occur.

In order to anticipate the procedures for estimation, suppose one suspected bias in a coin that was flipped—it seemed to result in more heads (H) than tails (T). Let the *probability* of an H be denoted by π. Suppose now that H resulted 65 times from 100 flips. The *estimate* of π, denoted $\hat{\pi}$, is $65/100 = 0.65$. Of course, the actual value of π is still unknown.

This tendency towards H may also be described in terms of the *odds* θ, where $\theta = \pi/(1-\pi)$. In this case, $\hat{\theta} = 65/(100-65) = 65/35 = 1.857$. The odds of H rather than T is about $1.857:1.0$. With $\hat{\pi} = 0.65$ ($\hat{\theta} = 1.857$), one might indeed believe that the coin is biased.

The estimate of $\pi(\theta)$ as a ratio of appropriate frequencies of outcomes depends on the outcomes being *replications governed by the same value* π. If they were not governed by the same value, then we could not use the simple method we have just used for estimating $\pi(\theta)$.

Statistical independence. The same calculations also depend on the replications being statistically independent in the sense that each contributes equivalently to the estimate. They must be independent, even though to help estimate the same value they also must be related. The outcomes are related by being governed by the same parameter.

Statistical *independence* is expressed by the principle that

$$\Pr\{O_1, O_2, O_3 \ldots O_i \ldots O_{100}\} = \Pr\{O_1\}\Pr\{O_2\}\Pr\{O_3\} \ldots \Pr\{O_i\} \ldots \Pr\{O_{100}\}$$

where O_i designates the outcome on the ith flip of the coin and Pr designates a probability.

Mean value estimates (MVE). Formally, if s is the frequency of H from N replications, then the model for the probability distribution of s is binomial, given by

$$\Lambda = \Pr\{s; N, \pi\} = \binom{N}{s} \pi^s (1-\pi)^{N-s} \qquad [1.1]$$

with $E[s] = N\pi$ where $E[s]$ is the expectation or theoretical mean of s.

In equation 1.1, π is the model *parameter.* Its estimate may be obtained by setting the observed s equal to the theoretical mean $E[s]$.

Thus $s = N\hat{\pi}$ and $\hat{\pi} = s/N$. This is the formula used intuitively in the coin example.

Maximum likelihood (ML) estimation. An alternative and important method of estimation is that of maximum likelihood. To obtain the maximum likelihood estimate of π from equation 1.1, we find the value of π that maximizes the observed number s. This is most easily accomplished by finding the value π that maximizes the logarithm of equation 1.1, which is permissible because the same value maximizes equation 1.1. Taking the logarithm gives

$$\log\Lambda = \log\Pr\{s; N, \pi\} = \log\binom{N}{s} + s\log\pi + (N - s)\log(1 - \pi) \quad [1.2]$$

Differentiating equation 1.2 with respect to π and setting it equal to 0 evaluates π at the maximum of equation 1.2:

$$\frac{\partial \log \Lambda}{\partial \pi} = \frac{s}{\hat{\pi}} - \frac{N - s}{1 - \hat{\pi}} = 0 \quad [1.3]$$

Upon simplification of equation 1.3, $\hat{\pi} = s/N$, as in the mean value estimation. MVE and MLE are not always the same, and, as we shall see, the latter procedure has certain advantages for application with Rasch models.

The above brief discussion must suffice to introduce some vocabulary and to set the Rasch model into a measurement context. Now we introduce an example which will be carried through the book.

Example 1.1. Responses of 1,697 persons in Western Australia to six items (questions) of Eysenck's Personality Inventory (1958) that pertain to neuroticism—Eysenck's Neuroticism Scale (ENS)—are shown in Table 1.1. The details by which Eysenck generated and constructed these items—that is, the frame of reference and the observation framework—will not be studied here. However, after exploring the data, we will return to consider some issues about the frame of reference that arise from the analysis.

Clearly, the questions are intended to be replications of some kind. Equally clearly, they have different frequencies of responses. If only one question had been asked, then a different mood may be inferred for the persons, depending on which question had been asked. One purpose in asking more than one question is to overcome this ambiguity in inter-

TABLE 1.1

Six Items of the Eysenck Personality Inventory that Pertain
to Neuroticism and Their Response Frequencies

Item	Response		
	Yes	No	Total
1. Do you sometimes feel happy, sometimes depressed without any apparent reason?	1241	456	1697
2. Do you have frequent ups and downs in mood, either with or without apparent cause?	826	871	1697
3. Are you inclined to be moody?	500	1197	1697
4. Does your mind often wander when you are trying to concentrate?	852	845	1697
5. Are you frequently "lost in thought," even when you are supposed to be taking part in a conversation?	650	1047	1697
6. Are you sometimes bubbling over with energy and sometimes very sluggish?	1184	513	1697

pretation. Account must be made, however, of the differences in the frequencies of responses.

In addition, we note that the intended way that the responses are to be combined is by simple summation of the yes responses. The greater the number of yes responses, the greater the neuroticism implied. Therefore, the model chosen for the analysis should express these intentions. It is stressed that *the model is chosen to express intentions, and not simply to describe the data that might be collected.* Whether the responses actually satisfy these intentions that the yes responses can be summed meaningfully is explored, then, by checking how closely they conform to the chosen model. Because more theory is required for that purpose, we leave the example now and return to it as the theory is developed.

Latent variables. It is important to appreciate that in making observations that reflect properties, the actual properties are not observed—only their manifestations are observed. The properties are abstractions based on the patterns of observations. We take the position that it turns out to be a very minor issue, if it is an issue at all, whether or not the property exists. The main issue is whether or not postulating the property and its operationalized form or forms is useful in understanding some related set of phenomena deemed to be important for some reason. Two further conventions emanate from this perspective. First, the properties postulated are often termed *constructs*; second, they are also often termed *latent traits* or *latent variables*.

Thus, in the ENS example, a latent variable of neuroticism is considered to be manifested by the responses, and different numbers of yes responses are taken to indicate different degrees of neuroticism.

Measurement models. Mathematical models are used to convert observations into measurements. Thus the model f = ma can be interpreted as a measurement model. An important form of the model for illustrative purposes is a = f/m, in which a is a function of f and m. The observations a are treated immediately as if they are continuous and the model is deterministic. In contrast, the responses in Table 1.1 are discrete and we need a statistical model to convert the observations into measurements.

Some features, however, will remain the same in both the deterministic and the statistical cases. In the case of a = f/m, it is evident that the acceleration a depends on both the mass of the object m and the force f that is imposed upon it. Rasch (1960/1980, 1977) supposed that some *agent* imposed this force. Analogously, in the case of the responses to the items of the ENS, it is expected that the response will depend, in part, on the degree of neuroticism of the individual. This neuroticism of a person corresponds to the mass of the object. In addition, from the evidence that the same group of people respond differently to the different items, it is reasonable to suppose that the items have characteristics that elicit neuroticism differently. This difference is a difference in *intensity*. Thurstone (1959), who pioneered the scaling and measurement of phenomena that have no physical counterpart, termed this characteristic of an item its *affective* value. Clearly, the different items in this context correspond to different forces.

Let the attitude of person n be characterized by the variable B_n and the affective value of item i be characterized by the variable D_i. The symbols B and D, respectively, represent the properties of attitude and affective value in general terms, but they can be used also as magnitudes for the properties. Here we use them in both senses. If we introduce the discrete variable X, which takes on the value x = 0 for one response (say, disagree) and x = 1 for the other (that is, agree), then the observed response x is governed (not determined) by B_n and D_i. Therefore, we write that the value x will be observed with a certain probability as a function of B_n and D_i in the following way:

$$\Pr\{X = x\} = \phi(B_n, D_n) \qquad [1.4]$$

where ϕ is some function. B_n and D_i are the parameters in the model. In order to estimate their values from observed data, it is necessary to specify ϕ.

Conclusion: Constructing a Variable

The construction of a variable thus requires (i) appreciating the possibility of summarizing some set of phenomena into a construct that can be thought of in terms of magnitudes, (ii) eliciting through an observation framework from within a specified frame of reference the relevant observations with adequate consistency, and (iii) the choice and application of a mathematical model to transform the observations into measurements.

This chapter was concerned primarily with introducing the general vocabulary, concepts, and perspectives to be used throughout the rest of the volume in describing the process of measuring.

2. FUNDAMENTAL MEASUREMENT

In the previous chapter, we took the concept of measurement for granted. That could be continued, but because the Rasch models have a special relationship to *fundamental measurement*, it is opportune to re-examine this very important idea. In so doing, note that Stevens's (1946) famous classification of levels of measurement is not adopted here. Duncan (1984) provides a detailed account of the confusion this system has brought to the quantitative social sciences.

There is another reason to broach the topic of fundamental measurement here. Most discussions of fundamental measurement are found in specialized literature in mathematical psychology, philosophy of science, or mathematics, and the social science researcher concerned with constructing measuring instruments is left with the impression that fundamental measurement is an ideal that social science cannot achieve. However, with the careful application of Rasch models, and by invoking the knowledge available for constructing sound tests and questionnaires, it is possible to *attempt* to construct measurements of a fundamental kind in standard test and questionnaire exercises. This volume is concerned with the rationale and technical procedures for checking whether such measurements have been achieved.

Concatenation. Below is a very abbreviated rendition of some ideas in fundamental measurement. Full discussions can be found in Ellis (1966), Krantz et al. (1971), and Roberts (1979). While fundamental measurement is a sophisticated concept, in its most elementary form it simply allows for arithmetic operations of addition and subtraction on measures. This operation corresponds to a concatenation or amalgamation of the objects measured, an operation taught in elementary schools. A one-to-one correspondence is established, or shown to be valid, between the structure of addition and subtraction on real numbers and the structure of the properties of the objects that are measured.

The measurement of mass is a familiar example of fundamental measurement. Objects may be pooled and the sum of their masses is the same as the mass of the pooled objects, and (within an appropriate frame of reference) the pooled objects behave as a new object with a mass that is the sum of the individual masses. By having addition that corresponds to amalgamation or concatenation of objects, a variable is defined over the range in which the addition can take place. A unit of mass that can be amalgamated successively can be defined; *importantly, this unit has the same meaning throughout the operating range of the variable.*

We have used the familiar example of the mass of an object and related it to both a mathematical model and the concept of fundamental measurement. Mass may appear tangible through its universal gravitational effects, though the separation of the mass from the force of gravity in Newtonian mechanics was a decisive step. Fundamental measures may, however, be constructed where the concatenation is not so literal: Measures of the familiar electric current is one such example, and the measurement of temperature, equally familiar, is even further removed from the possibility of interpreting concatenation. We will return to this aspect of fundamental measurement shortly, but first we observe another feature of these examples, a feature they have in common with our example of the ENS.

The two-way frame of reference. To have evidence of the degree of mass of an object, the effect of gravity may be harnessed or some other force applied to the object. To observe the degree of heat in an object, it must affect some other entity, such as liquid, which expands and contracts with the variation in the amount of heat. These complementary concepts (force and mass, heat and the expansion of a body) are, in fact, defined in terms of each other; they illustrate what philosophers of science (Barnes, 1982) term *constitutive definitions.* It may be useful to

TABLE 2.1
The Two-Way Frame of Reference

	Agents (forces)					Agents (items)			
	F_1	$F_2\cdots$	$F_i\cdots$	F_l		D_1	$D_2\cdots$	$D_i\cdots$	D_L
m_1	a_{11}	$a_{12}\cdots$	$a_{1i}\cdots$	a_{1L}	B_1	x_{11}	$x_{12}\cdots$	$x_{1L}\cdots$	x_{1L}
m_2	a_{21}	$a_{22}\cdots$	$a_{2i}\cdots$	a_{2L}	B_2	x_{21}	$x_{22}\cdots$	$x_{2i}\cdots$	x_{2L}
·	·	·	·	·	Objects	·	·	·	·
·	·	·	·	·	(persons)	·	·	·	·
·	·	·	·	·		·	·	·	·
m_n	a_{n1}	$a_{n2}\cdots$	$a_{ni}\cdots$	a_{nL}	B_n	x_{n1}	$x_{n2}\cdots$	$x_{ni}\cdots$	x_{nL}
·	·	·	·	·	·	·	·	·	·
·	·	·	·	·	·	·	·	·	·
·	·	·	·	·	·	·	·	·	·
m_N	a_{N1}	$a_{N2}\cdots$	$a_{Ni}\cdots$	a_{NL}	B_N	x_{N1}	$x_{N2}\cdots$	$x_{Ni}\cdots$	NL

NOTE: a = continuous reactions or responses; x = discrete outcomes or responses.

note that measurement follows theory (Kuhn, 1961; Hughes, 1980), and not the other way around.

The point to observe here is that it is necessary to have two classes of entities involved. In the ENS example, one class is that of persons (objects), the other is that of items (agents). The objects, agents, and their responses (discrete or continuous, depending on the case), when brought in contact, may be set up in a two-way frame of reference, as shown in Table 2.1. Table 2.1 shows both the example from physics and the example involving responses of persons to items. The frame of reference may require extension beyond the two-way, but the two-way is the frame of the smallest order for constructing measures and it is the one to which we confine ourselves in this volume.

Simultaneous conjoint measurement. It was noted above that there are examples (in physics) where the concatenation of objects is not literal. Luce and Tukey (1964) formalized this general form of fundamental measurement. They, too, began with a two-way frame of reference and demonstrated that a simultaneous scaling (transformation) of the two variables, together with the response variable, is required so that an additive structure results. They stressed that the scaling of the variables is *simultaneous*, and, because of the resultant additive structure, this form of measurement has also been termed *additive* conjoint measurement as well as simultaneous conjoint measurement (for example, Perline et al., 1979).

It may appear that when a measuring instrument is used, only the object is measured. In this case, however, the simultaneous scaling has been done earlier as part of the process of constructing the instrument and the measurement is on the scale of the original simultaneous scaling of the objects and the agents.

The example from physics that we have used involves a multiplicative structure, $a = f/m$, whereas we have drawn on the work of Luce and Tukey that refers to an additive structure. Providing additions and multiplications are not mixed up in expressions, the two are equivalent. (Having only additions or multiplications provides a group structure on either operation). Thus, by taking logarithms, $a = f/m$ may be transformed to $\log(a) = \log(f) - \log(m)$ or $A = F + M$ where $A = \log(a)$, $F = \log(f)$ and $M = -\log(m)$.

The significance of a multiplicative structure (or, equivalently, an additive structure) and fundamental measurement is brought out by Ramsay (1975) in his comprehensive review of Krantz et al. (1971). In two places in the review he refers to his relationship. First, in a brief description of the contents of Chapter 10 he writes:

This chapter is unique in considering the representation of relations between measurable structures explicitly. It deals with the remarkable fact that virtually all the laws of physics can be expressed numerically as multiplications or divisions of measurement [p. 258].

Second, he concludes his review with the following remarks:

The most challenging chapter in mind is the last; it confronts the remarkable fact throughout the gigantic range of physical knowledge numerical laws assume a remarkably simple form, provided fundamental measurement has taken place. Although the authors cannot explain this fact to their own statisfaction, the extension to behavioral science is obvious: We may have to await fundamental measurement before we will see any real progress in quantitive laws of behavior. In short, ordinal scales (even continuous ordinal scales) are perhaps not good enough and it may not be possible to live forever with a dozen different procedures for quantifying the same piece of behavior, each making strong but untestable and basically unlikely assumptions which result in nonlinear plots of one scale against another. Progress in physics would have been impossibly difficult without fundamental measurement, and the reader who believes that all that is at stake in the axiomatic treatment of measurement is a possible canonizing of one scaling procedure at the expense of others is missing the point. A rationalization of quantification may be a necessary precondition of Psychology as a Quantitative Rational Science [p. 262].

These strong statements by Ramsay are highlighted here because conditions that produce the multiplicative structures and fundamental measurement may be explained by a concept more primitive than that of measurement—that of an invariant comparison.

Invariant comparisons. Just as in fundamental measurement, where concatenation is literal, a key realization of simultaneous conjoint measurement is a constant unit across the range of the variable. Because of the additive relationship across the entire two-way frame of reference, comparisons can be made by subtracting numbers associated with the objects, and a particular difference has the same interpretation across the entire continuum in which the relationship has been shown to hold. Thus a difference of a mass of 2 pounds is the same amount whether it is obtained as a difference between 4 pounds and 2 pounds or between 400 pounds and 398 pounds. Comparison is a key concept in psychology and science (Miller, 1962), and the *invariance* of a comparison on measures is a key concept within fundamental measurement.

Another important feature of the additive structure is that comparisons within one class in the two-way frame of reference are independent of comparisons within the other class. Thus suppose that we have objects of mass m_1 and m_2, respectively, and that they are acted upon by agent 1 with force f_1. The relationship of the accelerations to the masses and the force, following the logarithmic transformation shown, is $A_{11} = F_1 + M_1$ and $A_{21} = F_1 + M_2$. Then, by subtraction, $A_{11} - A_{21} = M_1 - M_2$ in which the force F_1 has been eliminated. Thus, through the comparison of accelerations, and independently of which force is involved, masses can be compared. A parallel operation can be constructed for the comparison of two forces through the accelerations they impose on an object: The comparison between the two forces is independent of the mass of the object.

In some sense, the concept of a comparison precedes measurement. This point is presented well by Webb et al. (1969):

> In this discussion, we assume that the goal of the social scientist is always to achieve interpretable comparisons, and that the goal of methodology is to rule out those plausible rival hypotheses which make comparisons ambiguous and tentative.
>
> Often it seems that absolute measurement *is* involved, and that a social instance is being described in its splendid isolation, not for comparative purposes. But a closer look shows that the absolute, isolated measurement is meaningless. In all useful measurement, an implicit comparison exists when an explicit one is not visible [p . 5].

The invariance of comparisons, the additive structure, and the maintenance of the unit across a two-way frame of reference are all related to fundamental measurement. And, as we have seen, they form an integral part of the quantitative laws of classical physics. Without seeming to make too bold a claim in this introductory volume, it is possible that *the invariance of a comparison expressed in numerical form is the condition that answers Ramsay's question of why laws are multiplicative when measurement has taken place.* The reason for making such a claim is that the criterion of invariance of a comparison in the case of deterministic responses does lead necessarily to multiplicative or additive relationships of the kind found in physics (Rasch, 1977). In addition, the case for the Rasch model for probabilistic responses, which also has a multiplicative structure, rests on the invariance of appropriate comparisons.

The quantitative form of physical laws should not dictate the data collection and analysis of social science data. However, when the key features of a statistical model relevant to the analysis of social science data are the same as those of the laws of physics, then these features are difficult to ignore. As we shall see, this is the case with the Rasch model, and the above very brief sketch of some aspects of fundamental measurement is meant to give an orientation to the construction of variables from the perspectives of these models.

Example 2.1. We close this chapter by casting the example into a two-way frame of reference. The procedure is standard, but it will prove decisive that it can be justified by applying the Rasch model for simple dichotomous responses. This justification is made in Chapter 4.

Table 2.2 shows the data in the two-way form. The persons have been grouped according to their *total* scores on the six-item questionnaire and within the cells of the table are the numbers of persons with a given total score who have agreed to the item. This form of the table not only gives a two-way structure but also sets the stage for dealing with the responses probabilistically.

Two further points about this table must be highlighted. First, the items have been ordered according to the numbers of persons who agreed to them. Likewise, the score groups are ordered. Second, even though we have contrived a two-way table, the two sets of numbers in the margins are *not independent* of each other: If a number is changed in one of the margins, then a number is changed in the corresponding cell, and, consequently, so is a corresponding number in the other margin. Thus one margin cannot be treated as an independent variable the values of which are determined independently of the responses, and the other margin treated as a dependent variable that varies simply as a function of the independent variable. They must be treated jointly. Any transformations imposed will be *conjoint* in the sense of Luce and Tukey (1964).

Nevertheless, we may orient ourselves to the data by considering how agreement to each item varies as a function of the total score on the items. This is best done by converting the cell frequencies to proportions of the number of persons who obtained each total score. These proportions are also shown in Table 2.2, and we can see that the greater the total score, the greater the proportion of persons who agreed to any item.

TABLE 2.2
Responses to Six Items of the ENS Cast in a
Two-Way Frame of Reference

Score r	Frequency n_r	Item$_i$					
		1	6	4	2	5	3
0	308	.00 (0)	.00 (0)	.00 (0)	.00 (0)	.00 (0)	.00 (0)
1	318	.35 (112)	.36 (113)	.16 (50)	.04 (12)	.05 (17)	.04 (14)
2	352	.66 (232)	.59 (206)	.32 (113)	.18 (64)	.21 (73)	.05 (16)
3	298	.78 (231)	.77 (229)	.45 (134)	.47 (139)	.40 (119)	.14 (42)
4	295	.94 (277)	.86 (254)	.64 (188)	.76 (225)	.42 (124)	.38 (112)
5	219	.97 (212)	.94 (205)	.87 (190)	.95 (209)	.64 (140)	.63 (139)
6	177	1.00 (177)	1.00 (177)	1.00 (177)	1.00 (177)	1.00 (177)	1.00 (177)
Totals	s_i	1241	1184	852	826	650	500

NOTE: Observed proportions $p_{ri} = f_{ri}/n_r$ where f_{ri}(in parentheses) is the number of the n_r persons with a total score of r who agree to item i.

A graphical display of these proportions is shown in Figure 2.1. It can be seen that the differences in frequencies noticed when the example was introduced manifest themselves through the different locations of the graphs. These differences reflect different affective values of the items.

Cumulative data and models. The type of data revealed in Table 2.1 is said to be cumulative—the probability of a particular response varies monotonically as a function of the affective value of an item and the location of the person (or the properties of the object and the agent in general). This cumulative form is known more formally as monotonic, and monotonicity is required for transformations to produce measurements.

With the above orientations to both data analysis and simultaneous or additive conjoint measurement, we are ready to study the simplest of the Rasch models.

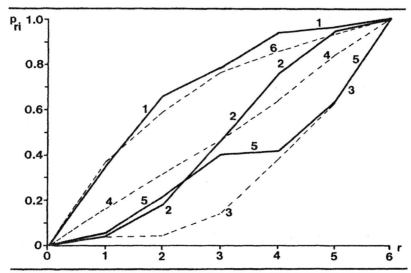

Figure 2.1: Proportions of Persons with a Total Score of r Who Agree to Item i

Conclusion

The basic element of measurement is a comparison, and the construction of measuring instruments provides special kinds of comparisons—quantitative ones. When fundamental measurement has taken place, relations among variables are invariably multiplicative or equivalently additive. And the comparisons among pairs of a class of objects are independent or invariant across the members of a class of agents with which they are brought in contact, and vice versa. Invariant comparisons are made in terms of a constant unit and each comparison is general across a range of values for the classes of objects and agents. Additivity, constant units, and invariant comparisons are all related, but the logic for the Rasch model begins, as we shall see in the next chapter, with the invariance of a comparison.

3. THE SIMPLE LOGISTIC MODEL

We specify here a cumulative model that is consistent with simultaneous conjoint measurement. In order to accomplish this, B and D of equation 1.4 are related to each other in an appropriate way, and a particular probability function ϕ is described. To accommodate the example introduced in Chapter 1, a statistical, rather than a deterministic, model is chosen immediately.

The parametric structure. Following the lead from the laws of physics, we specify a simple multiplicative or additive structure for relating B to D. Beginning with the multiplicative one, let

$$L_{ni} = B_n / D_i; \qquad B_n > 0, \; D_i > 0. \tag{3.1}$$

Taking logarithms gives the additive structure

$$\log L_{ni} = \log B_n - \log D_i, \quad \text{or} \quad \lambda_{ni} = \beta_n - \delta_i,$$

in which $\lambda = \log L$, $\beta = \log B$, and $\delta = \log D$. In the case of achievement testing, the location of the person, B or β, represents an ability and the scale value of the item, D or δ, represents its difficulty. In general, D is referred to as an item's *scale value* and B is referred to as a person's *location.*

The probability function. Now we specify the function ϕ:

Let

$$\phi(L_{ni}) = L_{ni} / (1 + L_{ni}) \tag{3.2}$$

Then

$$\Pr\{X_{ni} = 1\} = L_{ni} / (1 + L_{ni}) = (B_n / D_i) / G_{ni} \tag{3.3}$$

and

$$\Pr\{X_{ni} = 0\} = 1 / (1 + L_{ni}) = 1 / G_{ni}$$

in which $G_{ni} = 1 + B_n / D_i$ is a normalizing factor that ensures that $\Pr\{X_{ni} = 1\} + \Pr\{X_{ni} = 0\} = 1.0$. In addition, with $B_n > 0$ and $D_i > 0$, $0 < \Pr\{X_{ni} = 1\} < 1$ as required.

Equation 3.3 is one form of the Rasch model for dichotomous responses and in the form in which it is studied in the next chapter, it is known as the simple logistic model (SLM). The model is cumulative— as L_{ni} increases (that is, as B increases relative to D), the probability of the response $X_{ni} = 1$ also increases.

The odds formulation. An alternate specification of the model is in terms of odds.

The model $Pr\{X_{ni} = 1\} = L_{ni}/G_{ni} = (B_n D_i)/G_{ni}$ of equation 3.3 implies that $L_{ni} = B_n/D_i$ are the odds that person n scores 1 rather than 0 on item i. This can be seen from the ratio

$$\frac{Pr\{X_{ni} = 1\}}{Pr\{X_{ni} = 0\}} = \frac{L_{ni}/G_{ni}}{1/G_{ni}} = L_{ni} = B_n/D_i \qquad [3.4]$$

For example, if $B_n = 6$ and $D_i = 2$, then the odds that $X_{ni} = 1$ rather than 0 are 6:2. The probability that $X_{ni} = 1$ then is $6/(6 + 2) = 0.75$.

Estimation: Constructing Replications on a Pair of Items

Estimation is introduced by two approaches; one through the odds and the other through the probability formulation. Both approaches are used in the literature and so both will be broached here, although the latter will be given the main emphasis. Before proceeding, it is necessary to reintroduce the principle of statistical independence.

Statistical independence. If the response of a person to an item is governed only by fixed parameters, then with those parameters specified, the response of two persons n = 1 and n = 2 to a single item i are independent in the sense that

$$Pr\{X_{1i} = 1, X_{2i} = 1\} = Pr\{X_{1i} = 1\}Pr\{X_{2i} = 1\}$$

$$= (B_1/D_i)(B_2/D_i)/G_{1i}G_{2i} \qquad [3.5a]$$

Analogously, the responses of a single person n to two items i = 1 and i = 2 are independent in the sense that

$$Pr\{X_{n1} = 1, X_{n2} = 1\} = Pr\{X_{n1} = 1\}Pr\{X_{n2} = 1\}$$

$$= (B_n/D_1)(B_n/D_2)/G_{n1}G_{n2} \qquad [3.5b]$$

This case of a single person responding to two items is studied more closely now. To do so, consider the list of possible outcomes, called the *outcome space*, and their probabilities, shown in the top of Table 3.1.

Estimation through odds. Intuitively, response patterns $(0,0)$ and $(1,1)$, where the ordered pairs refer to the responses to items 1 and 2, respectively are uninformative for comparing the two items: The responses in each pattern are identical. On the other hand, responses $(1,0)$ and $(0,1)$ are different and are informative on *just that comparison.* Thus compare the probability of $(1,0)$ with the probability of $(0,1)$ in Table 3.1. This may be done using the *odds* ratio

$$\frac{\Pr\{(1,0)\}}{\Pr\{(0,1)\}} = \left(\frac{B_n/D_1}{B_n/D_2}\right)\left(\frac{G_{n1}\,G_{n2}}{G_{n1}\,G_{n2}}\right)$$

i.e., $\quad \dfrac{\Pr\{(1,0)\}}{\Pr\{(0,1)\}} = \dfrac{(1/D_1)}{(1/D_2)} = D_2/D_1 \qquad$ [3.6]

The significant feature of this ratio is that it does not contain the person parameter B! It has been eliminated. Thus the model ratio is the same for all persons and is independent of their locations B, which are different from person to person. Therefore, responses $(1,0)$ and $(0,1)$ *across all persons* can be considered *replications* and used to estimate the ratio D_2/D_1.

From the example shown in Table 3.1, the estimate $\hat{D}_2/\hat{D}_1 = 502/87 = 5.77$. Because the probability of the response 1 increases *inversely* as D in equation 3.3, item 2 is more than five times as intense as item 1: *If a person agrees to one of these two items only, then the odds that it is item 1 rather than item 2 are about 5.8:1.*

For completeness, in the logarithmic metric,

$$\log(\hat{D}_2/\hat{D}_1) = \log(502/87) = 1.75, \quad \text{i.e.,} \quad \hat{\delta}_2 - \hat{\delta}_1 = 1.75$$

Three points need to be highlighted. First, a numerical *comparison* between the scale values of the items has been made, either as a ratio or as a difference. Second, the comparison is independent of B; therefore, it is *invariant* across different sections of the continuum. Third, and analogously, the locations of two persons may be compared by their responses to many items independently of the scale values of the items.

28

TABLE 3.1
Probabilities of Responses of a Single Person n to Two Items and the Odds of Different Response Patterns

Example Frequencies	Response Patterns or Outcome Space Item 1	Item 2	Model Probabilities $\Pr\left\{x_{n1}, x_{n2}\right\}$
639	(0	0)	(1) $(1)/G_{n1}G_{n2}$
502	(1	0)	(B_n/D_1) $(1)/G_{n1}G_{n2}$
87	(0	1)	(1) $(B_n/D_2)/G_{n1}G_{n2}$
739	(1	1)	$(B_n/D_1)(B_n/D_2)/G_{n1}G_{n2}$
1967			

Example Odds Ratio	Conditional Outcome Space Item 1	Item 2	Model Odds Ratio
502/87	(1	0)	$\left(\dfrac{B_n/D_1}{G_{n1}G_{n2}}\right)/\left(\dfrac{B_n/D_2}{G_{n1}G_{n2}}\right)$
= 5.77	(0	1)	$= D_2/D_1$

Thus the procedure and the model satisfy the essentials of fundamental measurement. *The unit for the comparison is the odds (or the logarithm of the odds) of endorsing one item rather than the other when only one of the two items is endorsed.*

More will be made of the invariance of the comparison as the model is developed further. This development is enhanced through the probabilistic rather than the odds formulation.

Estimation through probabilities. Table 3.2 shows that the outcome space of Table 3.1 can be partitioned according to those responses that are identical and those that are different. This partitioning is summarized by the statistic $r_n = \Sigma_i x_{ni}$, the total score of the person on the two items. Table 3.2 also shows this partitioning of the outcome space according to the statistic r_n. Clearly, there is only one way of obtaining the scores $r_n = 0$ and $r_n = 2$, but there are two ways of obtaining the score $r_n = 1$.

Consider now the probability of obtaining one of the patterns, say (1,0), conditional on $r_n = 1$. This is obtained simply by dividing $\Pr\{(1,0)\}$ by $\Pr\{(r_n = 1)\}$; these probabilities are also shown in Table 3.2. Using the

TABLE 3.2
Probabilities of Responses of a Single Person n to
Two Items and the Conditional Probability of
Different Response Patterns

Example Frequencies	The Statistic $r = \sum_{i=1}^{2} n_{ni}$			Model Probability $\Pr\{r_n\}$
	Item 1	Item 2	r_n	
639	(0	0)	0	(1) $(1)/G_{n1}G_{n2}$
589	(1	0)	1	$(B_n/D_1 + B_n/D_2)/G_{n1}G_{n2}$
	(0	1)		
341	(1	1)	2	$(B_n/D_1)(B_n/D_2)/G_{n1}G_{n2}$

Example Proportions	Response Patterns Conditional on $r_n = 1$		Conditional Model Probabilities $\Pr\{x_{ni} = 1 \mid r_n = 1\}$
502/589 = 0.852	(1	0)	$D_2/(D_1 + D_2)$
87/589 = 0.148	(0	1)	$D_1/(D_1 + D_2)$

simplified notation below in which π_{12} indicates that the first item has the response 1 and the second 0, and in which | designates a conditioning on the restriction $r_n = 1$ that follows it,

$$\pi_{12} = \Pr\{(1, 0) \mid r_n = 1\} = \Pr\{X_{n1} = 1, X_{n2} = 0\}/\Pr\{r_n = 1\}$$

$$= \frac{(B_n/D_1)/G_{n1}G_{n2}}{(B_n/D_1 + B_n/D_2)/G_{n1}G_{n2}} = \frac{1/D_1}{1/D_1 + 1/D_2}$$

$$= (D_2/D_1)/(1 + D_2/D_1) = D_2/(D_1 + D_2) \qquad [3.7a]$$

Analogously,

$$\pi_{21} = \Pr\{(0, 1) \mid r_n = 1\} = (D_1/D_2)/(1 + D_1/D_2) = D_1/(D_1 + D_2) \quad [3.7b]$$

Equations 3.7 are equivalent to equation 3.6; equation 3.6 can be obtained directly as a ratio of equations 3.7a and 3.7b.

The estimation equation 3.7, as equation 3.6, does not involve a person parameter. *Thus, by considering only persons whose responses are either (1,0) or (0, 1), replications can be formed that are governed by the same parameter.* In this case, the parameter is a function only of D_1 and D_2.

The task of comparing the scale values of the items is in a form now equivalent to the coin example in Chapter 1. The two new dichotomous responses are $(1,0)$ and $(0,1)$; then, with N = the number of persons with $r = 1$, and s_1 = the number of persons who score $(1, 0)$,

$$\Pr\{s_1\} = \binom{N}{s_1} \pi_{12}^{s_1} (1 - \pi_{12})^{N-s_1}$$

giving

$$\hat{\pi}_{12} = s_1/N$$

In the example, N = 589 and s_1 = 502. Therefore $\hat{\pi}_{12}$ = 502/589 = 0.85. To obtain the ratio $\hat{D}_1/\hat{D}_2$ or the contrast $\hat{\delta}_1 - \hat{\delta}_2$ of the item parameters from $\hat{\pi}_{12}$, first convert π_{12} to odds:

$$\pi_{12} = (D_2/D_1)/(1 + D_2/D_1) \quad \text{and} \quad 1 - \pi_{12} = 1/(1 + D_2/D_1),$$

$$\therefore \pi_{12}/(1 - \pi_{12}) = D_2/D_1$$

In the example, $\hat{D}_2/\hat{D}_1$ = (502/589)/(1 − 502/589) = 502/(589 − 502) = 502/87 = 5.77, as before.

It is possible to carry out such a comparison between every pair of items. However, with many items, limitations of this method must be appreciated: First, the response frequencies can become very small and unstable in some of the cells; second, the frequencies are not independent from cell to cell; and third, therefore, the procedure is not suitable for checking directly how well the data accord with the model. Nevertheless, the comparison of items in pairs is important for two reasons, one of which will be discussed in the next chapter and the other in Chapter 5. Briefly, the approach provides a way of relating the model to the well-established literature on pair comparison methods and it also permits a ready way of handling missing data.

A constraint on the item parameters. The estimate obtained in the previous section was only of the ratio D_2/D_1 or of the contrast $\delta_2 - \delta_1$.

No unique value can be given for either of the item parameters. There-fore, it is conventional to impose the constraint $(\hat{D}_1)\,(\hat{D}_2) = 1.0$ on the two parameters, or equivalently $\hat{\delta}_1 + \hat{\delta}_2 = 0.0$. Then, with $\hat{D}_1\hat{D}_2 = 1.0$ and $\hat{D}_2/\hat{D}_1 = 5.77$, $\hat{D}_2^2 = 5.77$, giving $\hat{D}_2 = 2.40$ and $\hat{D}_1 = 0.42$. In the loga-rithmic metric, $\hat{\delta}_1 = -0.87$ and $\hat{\delta}_2 = 0.87$.

Maximum likelihood estimation. We look now at the ML method of estimation because it is the most popular method in the usual many-item case. In addition, because the logarithmic metric is used most com-monly, it is presented in that form. From equation 3.7a, with $\delta_i = \log D_i$,

$$\Pr\{(1,0)\,|\,r = 1\} = \exp(-\delta_1)/[\exp(-\delta_1) + \exp(-\delta_2)]; \qquad [3.8a]$$

$$\Pr\{(0,1)\,|\,r = 1\} = \exp(-\delta_2)/[\exp(-\delta_1) + \exp(-\delta_2)]; \qquad [3.8b]$$

Equations 3.8 can be combined into the single general form

$$\Pr\{(x_{n1}, x_{n2})\,|\,r = 1\} = \exp(-x_{n1}\delta_1 - x_{n2}\delta_2)/[\exp(-\delta_1) + \exp(-\delta_2)] \quad [3.9]$$

in which the observed response x appears as a coefficient of the param-eters. When $x_{n1} = 1$ (and $x_{n2} = 0$), equation 3.9 reduces to equation 3.8a; when $x_{n2} = 1$ (and $x_{n1} = 0$), equation 3.9 reduces to equation 3.8b.

If N persons have a score $r_n = 1$, and invoking statistical independence across persons, the probability of the observed data is

$$\lambda = \prod_n \Pr\{(x_{n1}, x_{n2})\,|\,r = 1\}$$

$$= \prod_n \exp(-x_{n1}\delta_1 - x_{n2}\delta_2)/[\exp(-\delta_1) + \exp(-\delta_2)]^N$$

$$= \exp[-\sum_n x_{n1}\delta_1 - \sum_n x_{n2}\delta_2]/[\exp(-\delta_1) + \exp(-\delta_2)]^N,$$

that is,

$$\lambda = \exp[-s_1\delta_1 - s_2\delta_2]/[\exp(-\delta_1) + \exp(-\delta_2)]^N \qquad [3.10]$$

in which $s_1 = \sum_n x_{n1}$ and $s_2 = \sum_n x_{n2}$ are the respective total number of times each item is chosen. In the example of two items, $s_1 = 502$, $s_2 = 87$, and $N = s_1 + s_2 = 589$. Therefore,

$$\log \lambda = -s_1\delta_1 - s_2\delta_2 - N\log[\exp(-\delta_1) + \exp(-\delta_2)]. \qquad [3.11]$$

Differentiating equation 3.11 with respect to δ_1 and δ_2, respectively, gives the solution equations

$$-s_1 + N \exp(-\delta_1)/[\exp(-\delta_1) + \exp(-\hat{\delta})] = 0,$$

$$\text{i.e.,} \quad -s_1 + N\hat{\pi}_{12} = 0, \qquad [3.12a]$$

$$\text{and} \quad -s_2 + N\hat{\pi}_{21} = 0 \qquad [3.12b]$$

Equations 3.12 are not independent, as can be demonstrated simply by taking their sum: This sum reduces to $-N + N = 0$. Therefore, the usual constraint $\hat{\delta}_1 + \hat{\delta}_2 = 0.0$ is introduced here. With only two items, these equations can be solved explicitly using the methods presented earlier, that is, by forming ratios of equations 3.12a and 3.12b. From equation 3.12a $\hat{\pi}_{12} = s_1/N$, the solution encountered earlier. In the general case, equations 3.12 must be solved iteratively. This method is described in Chapter 5.

Check on the model: invariance of the comparison. We have stressed the kind of invariance of the comparisons that the SLM provides for pairs of persons and pairs of items. This invariance, however, is a property of the model and it is an empirical matter whether or not the data conform to the model. Checking and exploring deviations from a model is dealt with in detail in Chapter 6, but before closing this chapter, its basics are introduced through the ENS example.

In the example, the ratio $\hat{D}_2/\hat{D}_1 = 5.77$ (or $\hat{\delta}_2 - \hat{\delta}_1 = 1.75$) has been estimated. This ratio does not involve the location B_n of any person. Therefore, if the data are consistent with the model, this ratio should be invariant across the continuum.

Example 3.1. To check the constancy of the ratio across the continuum, the ratios of frequencies of responses $(1,0)$ and $(0,1)$ at each *total* score are compared. Table 3.3 shows these frequencies for items 1 and 2 for the scores $r = 1, 2, 3, 4,$ and 5. The frequencies $(1, 0)$ and $(0, 1)$ are zero for $r_n = 0$ and $r_n = 6$. Figure 3.1 shows the graphical counterpart of Table 3.3.

To check whether the ratios shown in table 3.3 are statistically equivalent, the conventional χ^2 test used with contingency tables can be used: The χ^2 value on 4 degrees of freedom is 14.98. This is statistically significant at the 0.01 level, but the largest contribution by far to the χ^2—that of 8.02—comes from the cell with the small expected

TABLE 3.3
Odds Ratio for Items 1 and 2 for
Scores r_n = 1, 2, 3, 4, 5 in the ENS

Score r_n	Observed Frequencies			Expected Frequencies		
	(1, 0)	(0, 1)	Ratio	91, 0)	(0, 1)	Ratio
1	112	12	9.33	105.68	18.31	5.77
2	196	28	7.00	190.91	33.09	5.77
3	116	24	4.83	119.32	20.68	5.77
4	68	16	4.25	71.59	12.41	5.77
5	10	7	1.43	14.49	2.51	5.77
	502	87	5.77	502	87	5.77

$$\chi^2 = 14.98, \; df = 4, \; p < 0.05$$

frequency of 2.51. Also in Figure 3.1, the points tend to be located about the line that represents the overall ratio of the frequencies of responses (1,0) and (0,1). However, looking closely at Table 3.3, it might be noted that the ratio decreases as the scores of persons increase. Thus, at a general level, the ratios are quite close to a constant, but at a more

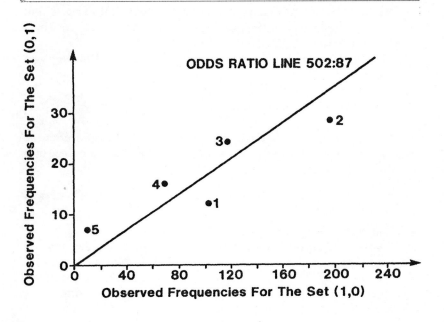

detailed level it can be seen that they deviate systematically from this constant.

Conclusion

The exposition in this chapter showed the basic features of the SLM. The next chapter presents the model in a more conventional form in which it is easier to estimate parameters and make tests of fit between the model and the data. The reader may have noted some features that are familiar to measurement and scaling advocated elsewhere. Because it is instructive to appreciate where the model is similar to other approaches, the next chapter also makes connections between the model and two well-known rationales for scale construction, those Guttman and Thurstone.

4. THE GENERAL FORM OF THE SLM AND THE GUTTMAN AND THURSTONE PRINCIPLES FOR SCALING

The first part of this chapter may appear technical in parts, but working through the expressions makes clear the natural role of a person's total score in the SLM.

The general form of the SLM. Writing equation 3.3 in the logarithmic metric,

$$\Pr\{X_{ni} = 1\} = \exp[(\beta_n - \delta_i)]/\gamma_{ni}; \qquad \Pr\{X_{ni} = 0\} = 1/\gamma_{ni} \qquad [4.1]$$

in which $\gamma_{ni} = 1 + \exp(\beta_n - \delta_i)$ is the normalizing factor. Incorporating the random variable X, the two parts of equation 4.1 may be combined into the single equation

$$\Pr\{X_{ni} = x_{ni}\} = \exp[x_{ni}(\beta_n - \delta_i)]/\gamma_{ni} \qquad [4.2]$$

in which $x_{ni} = 0$ or $x_{ni} = 1$.

The structure of equation 4.2 justifies the description of the model as the simple logistic (SLM): It is logistic because the function $f(\lambda) = \exp(\lambda)/(1 + \exp(\lambda))$ is the logistic; it is simple because it is the simplest parameterization for the simplest of responses, the dichotomous response. The contrast $\beta_n - \delta_i$ is, therefore, a logit.

It is common to build the parameters β_n and δ_i into the left of equation 4.2, even though their presence on the right makes them redundant. Mostly, this is done by writing

$$Pr\{X_{ni} = x_{ni} | \beta_n, \delta_i\} = exp[x_{ni}(\beta_n - \delta_i)]/\gamma_{ni} \qquad [4.3a]$$

in which | indicates that x_{ni} depends on β_n and δ_i. In this book, a different notation, ; , is used (as suggested by Graham Douglas in a personal communication), namely,

$$Pr\{x_{ni}; \beta_n, \delta_i\} = exp[x_{ni}(\beta_n - \delta_i)]/\gamma_{ni} \qquad [4.3b]$$

The conditional notation | is reserved for *conditioning on statistics*, an important feature of Rasch models. In addition, x_{ni} will be written without subscripts unless ambiguity results, and likewise, β_n and δ_i will not generally be retained on the left of equations such as equation 4.3.

Figure 4.1 provides a graph of $Pr\{x = 1; \beta_n, \delta_i\}$: Figure 4.1a shows the probability as a function of β_n with a fixed δ_i and Figure 4.1b shows it as a function of δ_i for a fixed β_n. In general, the values of an observable contrast, $\beta_n - \delta_i$, range between about −3.0 and +3.0 corresponding to probabilities of approximately 0.05 and 0.95, respectively. A feature of the SLM, which is clear from the symmetry of equation 4.2 and Figure 4.1, is that the person and item parameters have equal *conceptual* status.

The total score and sufficiency. It was shown in the last chapter that, for the case of two items, the statistic r_n partitioned the outcome space in such a way that the probability of a particular outcome, conditional on $r_n = 1$, was independent of the person parameter β_n. Such a statistic is *sufficient* for β_n because the distribution of outcomes, conditional on the subspace formed by the statistic, is independent of β_n. All information about β_n is captured in r_n. Sufficiency plays key roles in Rasch models and Rasch's view on this concept, introduced by R. A. Fisher, is available in Rasch (1960/1980). We now generalize the sufficient statistic to the case of many items.

Suppose there are L items. Then the probability of the vector $(x_{n1}, x_{n2}, \ldots x_{nL})$ is

$$Pr\{(x_{n1}, x_{n2} \ldots x_{nL})\} = Pr\{x_{n1}\} Pr\{x_{n2}\} \ldots Pr\{x_{nL}\}$$

$$= exp[x_{n1}(\beta_n - \delta_1)] exp[x_{n2}(\beta_n - \delta_2)] \ldots$$

36

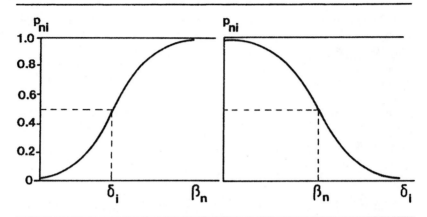

Figure 4.1a: Probability of a Positive Response $(P_r\{x = 1\})$ as a Function of β_n for Fixed δ_i

Figure 4.1b: Probability of a Positive Response $(P_r\{x = 1\})$ as a Function of δ_i for Fixed β_n

$$\exp[x_{nL}(\beta_n - \delta_L)]/\gamma_{n1}\gamma_{n2}\cdots\gamma_{nL}$$

$$= \exp[(x_{n1} + x_{n2} + \ldots x_{nL})\beta_n - x_{n1}\delta_1 - x_{n2}\delta_{n2}\cdots$$

$$-x_{nL}\delta_L]/\gamma_{n1}\gamma_{n2}\cdots\gamma_{nL}$$

$$= \exp[r_n\beta_n - \sum_i x_{ni}\delta_i]/\prod_i\gamma_{ni} \qquad [4.4]$$

in which $r_n = \sum_{i=1}^{L} x_{ni} = x_{n1} + x_{n2}\cdots x_{nL}$ is the total score of person n.

For example, if L = 3, then

$$\Pr\{(1, 1, 0)\} = \exp[2\beta_n - \delta_1 - \delta_2]/\gamma_{n1}\gamma_{n2}\gamma_{n3}$$

and

$$\Pr\{(1, 0, 1)\} = \exp[2\beta_n - \delta_1 - \delta_3]/\gamma_{n1}\gamma_{n2}\gamma_{n3}$$

In both cases above, $r_n = 2$ appears as the coefficient of β_n because two items have $x_{ni} = 1$. It did not matter that the same sum arose from a different response pattern.

Consider now the probability of any total score r_n. This is the sum of probabilities of all ways of obtaining r_n: From equation 4.4

$$\Pr\{r_n = x_{n1} + x_{n2} + \ldots x_{nL}\} = \sum_{(x)|r}^{r} \Pr\{x_{n1}\} \Pr\{x_{n2}\} \ldots \Pr\{x_{nL}\}$$

$$= \sum_{(x)|r} \exp[r_n\beta_n - \sum_i x_{ni}\delta_i] / \pi_i \gamma_{ni} \qquad [4.5]$$

in which $\Sigma_{(x)|r}$ is a summation over all possible vectors (x_{ni}) with the total $\Sigma_i x_{ni} = r_n$. For $L = 3$, these probabilities are shown in Table 4.1. For $r_n = 1, 2, \ldots L - 1$, there is more than one pattern; therefore, the probability of any pattern, conditional on r_n, can be formed. For $r_n = 0$ and $r_n = 1$, there is only one pattern; consequently a conditional probability is 1.0, and, therefore, uninformative.

As with two items, the conditional probability is given by dividing the probability of each pattern by the probability of r_n. In the case of three items—Table 4.1, for example—three patterns produce $r_n = 2$. Then, for example, $\Pr\{(1,1,0)|r_n = 2\} = \Pr\{(1,1,0)\}/\Pr\{r_n = 2\}$

$$= \frac{\exp[2\beta_n - \delta_1 - \delta_2]/\gamma_{n1}\gamma_{n2}\gamma_{n3}}{\{\exp[2\beta_n - \delta_1 - \delta_2] + \exp[2\beta_n - \delta_1 - \delta_3] + \exp[2\beta_n - \delta_2 - \delta_3]\}/\gamma_{n1}\gamma_{n2}\gamma_{n3}}$$

that on simplification, in which the γ_{ni}s and βs are eliminated, gives

$$\Pr\{(1,1,0)|r_n = 2\} = \frac{\exp[-\delta_1 - \delta_2]}{\exp[-\delta_1 - \delta_2] + \exp[-\delta_1 - \delta_3] + \exp[-\delta_2 - \delta_3]} \qquad [4.6]$$

Generalizing equation 4.6 as the ratio of equations 4.4 and 4.5 gives

$$\Pr\{(x_{ni})|r_n\} = \exp[-\sum_i x_{ni}\delta_i]/\gamma_r \qquad [4.7]$$

in which

$$\gamma_r = \sum_{(x)|r} \exp[-\sum_i x_{ni}\delta_i]$$

TABLE 4.1
Probabilities of Vectors for $L = 3$ Items

| Items | | | Total Score | |
1	2	3	r_n	$\Pr\{r_n\}$
0	0	0	0	$1/\gamma_{n1}\gamma_{n2}\gamma_{n3}$
1	0	0		$\exp[\beta_n - \delta_1]/\gamma_{n1}\gamma_{n2}\gamma_{n3}$
0	1	0	1	$+ \exp[\beta_n - \delta_2]/\gamma_{n1}\gamma_{n2}\gamma_{n3}$
0	0	1		$+ \exp[\beta_n - \delta_3]/\gamma_{n1}\gamma_{n2}\gamma_{n3}$
1	1	0		$\exp[2\beta_n - \delta_1 - \delta_2]/\gamma_{n1}\gamma_{n2}\gamma_{n3}$
1	0	1	2	$+ \exp[2\beta_n - \delta_1 - \delta_3]/\gamma_{n1}\gamma_{n2}\gamma_{n3}$
0	1	1		$+ \exp[2\beta_n - \delta_2 - \delta_3]/\gamma_{n1}\gamma_{n2}\gamma_{n3}$
1	1	1	3	$\exp[3\beta_n - \delta_1 - \delta_2 - \delta_3]/\gamma_{n1}\gamma_{n2}\gamma_{n3}$

$$\gamma_{ni} = 1 + \exp(\beta_n - \delta_i)$$

is the elementary symmetric function of order r in the parameters (δ_i). In the case of three items,

$$\gamma_1 = \exp[-\delta_1] + \exp[-\delta_2] + \exp[-\delta_3] \qquad [4.8a]$$

and

$$\gamma_2 = \exp[-\delta_1 - \delta_2] + \exp[-\delta_1 - \delta_3] + \exp[-\delta_2 - \delta_3] \qquad [4.8b]$$

Specific values are illustrated in the next section.

Equation 4.7 reveals two crucial properties of the total score r_n. First, because β_n has been eliminated, the resultant probability distribution depends only on the δ_is: *All persons with the same total score, irrespective of their unknown β_n, provide replications with respect to only the item parameters.* Second, r_n contains all the information about a person's location. Consequently, the classification of persons according to their total scores is justified. Therefore the model is consistent with the intention of the ENS example in that the total score characterizes a person's neuroticism. Furthermore, as will be seen later, the total score is in one-to-one correspondence with $\hat{\beta}_n$.

It should be evident from the symmetry in the SLM that the total item score $s_i = \Sigma_n x_{ni}$ is a sufficient statistic for δ_i. (While the parameters β_n and δ_i have specific sufficient statistics in the sense that conditioning on each explicitly eliminates the corresponding parameter, it is considered generally that the set $\{(r_n), (s_i)\}$ provides jointly sufficient statistics.) In addition to (s_i) being sufficient for (δ_i), the estimates $(\hat{\delta}_i)$ are in one-to-one correspondence with (s_i). Accordingly, the ordering of items by their total scores is also consistent with the model. Thus the ordering of persons and items in Chapter 3 according to their total scores is justified by SLM.

The elimination of the person parameters when estimating the item parameters also means that the estimates $\hat{\delta}_i$ are independent of the unknown values β_n of the persons. Therefore, they are independent of the distribution of β in the sample or population available: The distribution of β does not have to be assumed to be normal or any other shape. Symmetrically, the estimates $\hat{\beta}_n$ are independent of the values of δ_i; therefore, it is unnecessary to assume that δ_i are spread uniformly or according to any other shape.

We continue the estimation in the next chapter, beginning with equation 4.7. For the rest of this chapter, we relate properties of the SLM to the established scaling rationales of Guttman and Thurstone (McIver and Carmines, 1981).

Relationships to Guttman Scaling. The joint ordering of persons and items draws attention to the Guttman Scale (Guttman, 1950; 1954). However, in contrast to the SLM, the response pattern in a perfect Guttman scale, given r_n, is completely determined. This pattern is shown in Table 4.2.

Because the restrictive Guttman pattern is hard to achieve, Guttman proposed some ad hoc methods for reproducing the patterns, given r_n. Through equation 4.7, ad hoc methods are obviated in the SLM because the probability of every pattern, conditional on r_n, is explicit—*the probability depends only on the relative scale values of the items.*

Table 4.3 illustrates the probabilities of all patterns, conditional on r_n for three items with $\delta_1 = 1.5$, $\delta_2 = -0.5$, and $\delta_3 = 2.0$. Notice the following three points: First, for each r_n, each pattern has a probability; second, the Guttman pattern has the greatest probability; and third, the probabilities are not symmetrical for the case of $r = 1$ and $r = 2$. This asymmetry results because the (δ_i) are not equally spaced. Accounting for differences in scale values is a major relaxation, and therefore improvement, over the Guttman criterion, while its intention is retained. The scale values affect the probabilities of patterns: The closer the scale values, the more likely that the extreme deterministic Guttman pattern will be violated, and vice versa.

TABLE 4.2
The Guttman Patterns for Three Items

	Items			
Responses	1	2	3	r_n
Acceptable	0	0	0	0
	1	0	0	1
	1	1	0	2
	1	1	1	3
Unacceptable	0	1	0	1
	0	0	1	1
	1	0	1	2
	0	1	1	2

TABLE 4.3
Response Matrix of All Possible Responses Partitioned
According to Total Scores and Their Respective Conditional
Probabilities for Three Items with Specified Scale Values

Item			Total Score	Probabilities
1	2	3	r	Pr $(x) \mid r$
0	0	0^a	0	1.00
1	0	0^a	1	0.72
0	1	0	1	0.26
0	0	1	1	0.02
				1.00
1	1	0^a	2	0.90
1	0	1	2	0.07
0	1	1	2	0.03
				1.00
1	1	1^a	1	1.00

NOTE: Hypothetical location values are $\delta_1 = -1.5$, $\delta_2 = -0.5$, $\delta_3 = 2.0$.
a. Patterns that belong to the Guttman scale.

These technical parallels between the SLM and the Guttman scale are not a coincidence. The connections arise from the same essential conditions required in both, including the requirement of invariance of scale and location values with respect to each other. According to Guttman (1950):

A person's score tells what his responses were to each question. . . . A person with a higher score is "favourable" on all questions that a person with a lower score answers "favourably," and on at least one more in addition. This rank order, furthermore, exists not only for the given series of questions, but is the same as the rank order that would be obtained with any other series of questions in the same area. . . .

While it is possible to get a rank order in nonscalable areas by assigning arbitrary weights to the items, this rank order does not possess the important invariant properties of a rank order where the problem of how much to weight each item does not occur [p. 20].

Some types of persons can be more numerous than other types, and/or some types of items can be more numerous than other types of items. The rank scores of people can have a binomial, Poisson, or any other distribution whatsoever as well as the uniform distribution we have used for illustration, and the types of items can also have an arbitrary distribution [p. 325].

In addition to the issue of invariance, Guttman (1950) considered he had refined the concept of unidimensionality: "Our definition of a single continuum as a series of items each of which is a simple function of the scale scores permits a clear-cut statement of what is meant by a rank order based on a single variable" (p. 154). The above quotes must suffice to indicate the similarity of Guttman's and Rasch's aims when constructing measures. Andrich (1985) discusses further the relationship between Rasch models and the Guttman Scale.

Relationships to Thurstone Scaling. Prior to the work of Guttman or Rasch, Thurstone (1926, 1927a, 1927b, 1927c) pioneered the construction of variables that have no physical counterpart, particularly those for the measurement of attitude and achievement. (Many of his papers have been reproduced in Thurstone, 1959.) Thurstone also was concerned with issues of dimensionality and invariance. On dimensionality, he wrote the following:

When we discuss opinions, about prohibition, for example, we quickly find that these opinions are multidimensional, that they cannot all be represented in a linear continuum. The various opinions cannot be completely described merely as "more" or "less." They scatter in many dimensions, but the very idea of measurement implies a linear continuum of some sort, such as length, price, volume, weight, age. When the idea of measurement is applied to scholastic achievement, for example, it is necessary to force the qualitative variations into a scholastic linear scale of some kind.

And so it is also with attitudes. We do not hesitate to compare them by the "more or less" type of judgment. We say about a man, for example, that he is more in favor of prohibition than some other, and the judgment conveys its meaning very well with the implication of a linear scale along which people or opinions might be allocated [Thurstone, 1928; 1959: 218-219].

It is evident that Thurstone appreciated the need to *construct* unidimensional variables and recognized the relative nature of unidimensionality. On invariance, he wrote the following:

If the scale is to be regarded as valid, the scale values of the statements should not be affected by the opinions of the people who help construct it. This may turn out to be a severe test in practice, but the scaling method must stand such a test before it can be accepted as being more than a description of the people who construct the scale [Thurstone, 1928, 1959: 228].

Thurstone also recognized the symmetry between persons and items in these requirements of invariance. In the context of achievement testing, he wrote that

it should be possible to omit several test questions at different levels of the scale without affecting the individual score [Thurstone, 1926: 446].

Much of Thurstone's work was based on his five cases of the law of comparative judgment for the pair comparison design in which every item was compared with every other item. There is a close relationship between the pair comparison design of the law of comparative judgment and the SLM. When the cumulative normal response process used by Thurstone is replaced by the numerically equivalent logistic process, Thurstone's most commonly applied case V of the law of comparative judgment is identical to the conditional equation 3.9 from which the relative scale values of a pair of items can be estimated (Andrich, 1978). In both cases, the person parameters are eliminated. Equation 3.9 gives the basis for the equivalence, because when the response is positive to only one of the items and negative to the other, the equivalent of a choice of one item ahead of the other can be inferred. Equation 3.9 is also identical to the Bradley-Terry-Luce (BTL) model for pair comparisons (Bradley and Terry, 1952; Luce, 1959). The model reflects the cumulative process in that it is expected that every person, no matter what his or her location, will be more likely to indicate that the same item of a pair has the greater intensity or affective value.

While Thurstone formalized a stochastic model for pair comparisons for items, he did not formalize the measurement of persons. Instead, he simply took as the measurement the mean or median of the scale value of the items the person endorsed. In this case, the responses were taken to be of the *unfolding* kind in the sense that a person tended to agree to items close in scale value to the person's location, and tended to reject items further away, irrespective of direction (Coombs, 1964; McIver and Carmines, 1981).

This unfolding process is different from the cumulative one specified by Guttman and Rasch. In aptitude or achievement testing, however, Thurstone did use the cumulative principle but tended to locate groups rather than individuals.

Specifically objective comparisons. The requirements set by Thurstone, Guttman, and Rasch for constructing measurements are consistent. In particular, the demand for invariance of comparisons across a scale that is unidimensional is paramount. Rasch differed from Thurstone in that he formalized an *individual* rather than a group location parameter, and he used the logistic rather than the normal distribution. He differed from Guttman in that he dealt with a formal probabilistic model in which persons and items were both parameterized.

Rasch articulated the conditions that give rise to measurement as follows:

> The comparison between two stimuli should be independent of which particular individuals were instrumental for the comparison; and it should also be independent of which other stimuli within the considered class were or might also have been compared.

> Symmetrically, a comparison between two individuals should be independent of which particular stimuli within the class considered were instrumental for comparison; and it should also be independent of which other individuals were also compared, on the same or on some other occasion [Rasch, 1961: 322].

Rasch's conditions are more complete than Thurstone's and Gutt-man's in that they appear as one simple set of conditions which have formal mathematical counterparts that show how the person or the item parameters can be eliminated explicitly. From Rasch's requirement of invariant comparisons, the SLM for dichotomous responses follows directly (Rasch, 1961, 1968). Here, Rasch stressed the separation of parameters for the motivation to the model. Wright and Douglas (1986) provide two elegant derivations based on the same requirement.

The SLM has been derived in other ways: Roskam and Jansen (1984) begin with a dominance relation between persons and items that satisfies a Guttman structure, while Andersen (1977) commences with the require-ment of a sufficient statistic for the person parameters. In both cases, the SLM is the only model that follows.

To identify models that permitted the separation of parameters as in the SLM, Rasch (1977) termed them *specifically objective: objective* because any comparison of a pair of parameters was independent of any other parameters or comparisons; *specifically objective* because the com-parison made was relative to some *specified frame of reference.*

Conclusion

This chapter provided the general form of the SML and set up the conditional equation for estimating the item parameters. This equation also demonstrated the property of sufficiency of the total score for the person location parameter and the invariance of the item scale values across the continuum. The chapter drew attention to the relationships between the scaling objectives of Rasch and those of Thurstone and Guttman and showed that they are all directed to similar ends.

5. ESTIMATION

Three methods of parameter estimation based on maximum like-lihood (ML) principles are studied in this chapter. Fischer (1981) establishes the conditions for the existence of ML estimates for the SLM. The first method described is the best theoretically, but is rela-tively inefficient computationally. The second is very efficient but requires some correction to the estimates. The third involves considering responses to items in pairs and approximating ML conditions. This method is also very efficient and is particularly appropriate for use with missing data.

Many programs exist for estimating the parameters of the SLM (Allerup and Sorber, 1977; Gustafsson, 1977; Wright and Mead, 1976), and the algorithms have been studied and discussed in specialized presentations dealing with the computations (Wright and Panchapakesan, 1969; Wright and Douglas, 1977; Andersen, 1972; Gustafsson, 1980a). Therefore, only the general principles will be considered here. Working through the basic equations of the methods is necessary to understand why different methods are employed. A small artificial example involving 10 persons and three items (shown in Table 5.1a) is presented. (Tables for the artificial example contain "a" in their numbering.)

Symmetry in the SLM—asymmetry in the data. First, note that, while person and item parameters are symmetrical conceptually in the SLM, empirically they have asymmetric status. Usually, a set of items is constructed for application to a class of persons. Then, from the responses of a sample of persons generally much greater in size than the number of items, the properties of items are determined. Some items than may be refined or modified. This step has been termed *item calibration* (Wright and Panchapakesan, 1969; Wright, 1977). After items have been calibrated, the locations of persons who respond to the test can be estimated. This stage is called *person measurement.*

Conditional estimation. We commence the estimation using the conditional equation 4.7. Because of independence, the conditional probability of the responses of all persons is given by the product of the individual probabilities:

$$\Lambda = \prod_{n=1}^{N} \Pr\{(x_{ni}) \mid r_n\} = \exp[-\sum_i \sum_n x_{ni}\delta_i] / \prod_{n=1}^{N} \gamma_r \qquad [5.1]$$

$$= \exp[\sum_i - s_i\delta_i] / \prod_{n=1}^{N} \gamma_r \qquad [5.2]$$

where $s_i = \sum_n x_{ni}$. The denominator of equation 5.2 may be simplified by noting that only persons whose scores are between 1 and $L - 1$ are retained. Combining the n_r persons with scores r_n gives

$$\prod_{n=1}^{N} \Pr\{(x_{ni}) \mid r_n\} = \exp[-\sum_i s_i\delta_i] / \prod_{r=1}^{L-1} \gamma_r^{n_r}. \qquad [5.3]$$

In the artificial example of Table 5.1a,

$$\Lambda = \exp[-7\delta_1 - 5\delta_2 - 3\delta_3]/\gamma_1^5 \, \gamma_2^5$$

Differentiating log L with respect to (δ_i), and setting the resultant equations equal to zero, gives the values of $\hat{\delta}_i$ that maximize Λ. After simplification[1] (see Appendix A), the general solution equation is

$$-s_i + \sum_{r=1}^{L-1} n_r \hat{\pi}_{ri} = 0, \qquad i = 1, 2 \ldots L, \qquad [5.4]$$

in which $\pi_{ri} = \Pr\{x_{ni} = 1 ; (\delta_i)|r\}$ is the probability that a person with a score of r obtains $x_{ni} = 1$ on item i. Equation 5.4 is an intuitively appealing equation: It shows that the estimated (proportion $\hat{\pi}_{ri}$) probability of persons with a score of r, times the number of persons with that score, when added over all persons, gives the total score of the item. For example, consider item 1 of Table 5.1a. The probability that a person with a score of r = 2 scores 1 on item 1 (and therefore a 1 on either one or the other of items 2 and 3, but not on both) is given from equation 4.6:

$$\pi_{21} = \Pr\{(1, 1, 0)|r = 2\} + \Pr\{(1, 0, 1)|r = 2\}$$

$$= \exp[(-\delta_1 - \delta_2) + \exp(-\delta_1 - \delta_3)]/\gamma_2 \qquad [5.5a]$$

Similarly,

$$\pi_{11} = \Pr\{(1, 0, 0)|r = 1\} = [\exp(-\delta_1)]/\gamma_1 \qquad [5.5b]$$

Inserting the estimated values for δ_i shown in Table 5.1a into equations 5.5 to give $\hat{\pi}_{11}$ and $\hat{\pi}_{21}$, and then substituting in the solution equation 5.4 shows that

$$-s_1 + [n_1\pi_{11} + n_2\pi_{21}] = -7 + 5(2.77) + 5(4.23) = 0.00, \text{ as required.}$$

In solving the L equations of equations 5.4, it must be appreciated that the usual constraint $\Sigma_{i=1}\delta_i = 0$ is imposed. The estimates δ_i in Table 5.1a do sum to 0.00.

TABLE 5.1a

Artificial Example of 10 Persons Responding to 3 Items
(Persons with $r_n = 0$ or $r_n = 3 = L$ are considered
already edited out of the data matrix)

Persons (n)	Total Score (r_n)	Responses to Items			Number of Persons n_r with a Total Score r
		1	2	3	
1	1	1	0	0	
2	1	1	0	0	
3	1	1	0	0	$n_1 = 5$
4	1	0	1	0	
5	1	0	1	0	
6	2	1	1	0	
7	2	1	1	0	
8	2	1	0	1	$n_2 = 5$
9	2	1	0	1	
10	2	0	1	1	
	s_i	7	5	3	

Conditional Estimates	$\hat{\delta}_i$	−0.640	0.000	0.640	$\sum_i \hat{\delta}_i = 0.00$

$\hat{\pi}_{ri}$		1	2	3	n_r
r	1	0.5539	0.2921	0.1540	5
	2	0.8460	0.7079	0.4461	5
	s_i	7	5	3	

Solution algorithms and standard errors. Equations 5.4 must be solved iteratively. The most direct procedure is the multiparameter Newton-Raphson method with obvious initial estimates that assume all β_n are zero, giving $\delta_i(0) = \log[(N - s_i)/s_i]$. We will not go into the detail of this solution algorithm, called here the conditional (CON) algorithm, but as part of it, it requires either the second derivative $\partial^2 \log \Lambda / \partial \delta_i^2$ for each item, or the matrix of second derivatives $\partial^2 \log \Lambda / \partial \delta_i \partial \delta_j$, where the former is generally used rather than the latter because it requires less computer storage. However, in maximum likelihood theory the estimate of the variance of the estimate in the single-parameter case is given by the negative inverse of the second derivative, while in the multiparameter case it is given by the negative of the diagonal of the inverse of the matrix of second derivatives. Therefore, as a by-product of the algorithm, standard errors are estimated. The approximation used in the more common approach, in which each item is solved for separately, results, on simplification, in

$$\hat{\delta}_i^2 = 1/ \sum_{r=1}^{L-1} n_r \hat{\pi}_{ri}(1 - \hat{\pi}_{ri}) \qquad [5.6]$$

from which the standard error of the estimate is given by $\hat{\delta}_i$.

The small number of items compared to the number of persons generally means that it is not practical to group items by their total scores to estimate the β_n. Instead, the δ_i are considered to be estimated sufficiently accurately that they are taken as shown when the person parameters are estimated. The estimation of person parameters arises from the second method of estimation, and therefore it is discussed in that context.

Example continued. Table 5.1 shows the conditional estimates for the six item parameters of the ENS, obtained by the CON algorithm. (It also shows estimates using the other procedures, and they will be referred to later.) The values are consistent with the frequencies of endorsement of items shown in Table 1.1: $\hat{\delta}_1$ has the lowest value and item 1 is the most frequency endorsed, while $\hat{\delta}_3$ has the greatest value and item 3 is the least frequently endorsed.

Interpreting the continuum. Figure 5.1 shows the items and their placement on a continuum according to the $\hat{\delta}_i$. To define the continuum, it is necessary that the items have different affective values.

Clearly, all items refer to swings in disposition, but, apparently, being sometimes happy and sometimes depressed without apparent cause (item 1) is much more readily endorsed than having frequent ups and downs in mood, with or without apparent cause (item 2), while being moody (item 3) is endorsed the least. It seems that the term *mood* has a particular potency, so that being moody reflects greater neuroticism than simply having changes in disposition from being happy to being depressed. A similar interpretation arises from the location of item 5, which refers to being lost in thought.

A critical test of validity for this post hoc interpretation of the continuum would be to construct further items and to predict their δ_i values. In addition, clinical assessments of individuals with different responses are necessary to establish validity.

Joint estimation. In joint ML estimation, the probability of the observed data matrix $[x_{ni}]$, $n = 1, N$; $i = 1, L$ is used. Thus

TABLE 5.1
Item Parameter Estimates by the Conditional, Joint,
and Pair-Wise Estimation Procedures in the ENS

Item	Conditional		Joint (Corrected)		Pair-Wise	
	$\hat{\delta}_i$	$\hat{\sigma}_i$	$\hat{\delta}_i$	$\hat{\sigma}_i$	$\hat{\delta}_i$	$\hat{\sigma}_i$
1	−1.17	.06	−1.19	.07	−1.18	0.06
2	0.13	.06	0.14	.06	0.14	0.06
3	1.26	.07	1.28	.07	1.30	0.07
4	0.05	.06	0.06	.06	0.02	0.06
5	0.71	.06	0.71	.06	0.66	0.06
6	−0.98	.06	−1.00	.06	−0.94	0.06

$$\Lambda = \Pr\left\{[x_{ni}] ; (\beta_n), (\delta_i)\right\} = \prod_n \prod_i \exp(x_{ni}(\beta_n - \delta_i))/\prod_n \prod_i \gamma_{ni} \qquad [5.7]$$

The log likelihood

$$\log \Lambda = \sum_n \beta_n r_n - \sum_i \delta_i s_i - \sum_n \sum_i \log(1 + \exp(\beta_n - \delta_i)),$$

in which $r_n = \sum_i x_{ni}$ and $s_i = \sum_n x_{ni}$, is then obtained readily. Differentiating $\log \Lambda$ with respect to δ_i and β_n and setting the result equal to 0.0 provides, on simplification, the two sets of solution equations

$$-s_i + \sum_{r=1}^{L-1} n_r \hat{\pi}_{ri} = 0, \qquad i = 1, 2 \ldots L, \qquad [5.8a]$$

and

$$r_n - \sum_i \hat{\pi}_{ni} = 0, \qquad n = 1, 2 \ldots N, \qquad [5.8b]$$

in which

$$\hat{\pi}_{ni} = \Pr\left\{x_{ni} = 1\right\} = \exp(\hat{\beta}_n - \hat{\delta}_i)/(1 + \exp(\hat{\beta}_n - \hat{\delta}_i)) \qquad [5.8c]$$

Like equations 5.4, equations 5.8 are implicit and therefore must be solved iteratively. In this iterative algorithm, the solution equations 5.8 are modified as follows. First, from equation 5.8b and from the sufficiency property of r_n, it is recognized that every person with the same total score will have the same *estimate* $\hat{\beta}_n$. (Note, it is the same estimate,

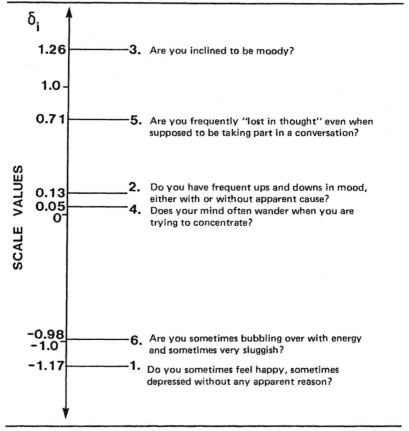

Figure 5.1: Scale Value of Eysenck's Neuroticism Items

not the same location β.) Therefore, equation 5.8b needs to be solved only for each total score r. In addition, collapsing the summation over all persons to one across all possible score groups in equation 5.8a gives

$$-s_i + \sum_{r=1}^{L-1} n_r \hat{\pi}_{ri} = 0, \qquad i = 1, 2 \ldots L, \qquad [5.9a]$$

$$r - \sum_i \hat{\pi}_{ri} = 0, \qquad r = 1 \ldots L-1, \qquad [5.9b]$$

together with the equation which sets the origin,

$$\sum_{i=1}^{L} \hat{\delta}_i = 0, \qquad\qquad [5.9c]$$

as the set of solution equations. In equations 5.9, note that (i) $\hat{\pi}_{ri} = \exp(\hat{\beta}_r - \hat{\delta}_i) / \hat{\gamma}_{ri}$; (ii) $\hat{\beta}_r$ is the estimate of the location parameter of any person with a total score of r, and (iii) $\hat{\gamma}_{ri} = 1 + \exp(\hat{\beta}_r - \hat{\delta}_i)$. Equation 5.9a cannot be solved for $s_i = 0$ or N and equation 5.9b cannot be solved for r = 0 or L.

The algorithm described above is very efficient and executes much more quickly than the conditional algorithm that solves equation 5.4. In North America and other English-speaking countries, most programs written for routine data analysis according to the SLM use the joint estimation procedure.

Notice that the conditional estimation equation 5.4 and the joint estimation equation 5.9a have an identical structure. However, the calculation of $\hat{\pi}_{ri}$ is different. In the CON estimation, $\hat{\pi}_{ri}$ is the probability that a person with a score of r obtains $x_{ni} = 1$ with the β_n of the person conditioned away, but dependent on *all item* parameters. In the joint procedure, $\hat{\pi}_{ri}$ represents the same probability, but with only the difficulty of item i and the *ability* $\hat{\beta}_r$ that, however, is estimated through the scale values of all the item parameters.

Person parameters. In the joint procedure, an ability estimate β_r is obtained from equation 5.9b for each total score, r = 1, L – 1, irrespective of whether or not any person in the sample actually obtained that total score. Also, equation 5.9b can be solved independently of equation 5.9a, given the item parameters. It is, in fact, the equation used to estimate person parameters when the item parameters have been estimated first by using the conditional procedure.

While the joint procedure is efficient, it has the weakness that for a fixed number of items the item parameters are inconsistent (Andersen, 1973). That is, for a fixed number of items, and even with increases in the number of persons, the item parameter estimates do not converge to their actual values. Wright and Douglas (1977) discuss this in detail and demonstrate that an accurate correction is to multiply the $\hat{\delta}_i$ by $(L - 1)/L$. Clearly, as L increases, the correction factor has a smaller effect, and this is in accord with Haberman's (1977) demonstration that as *both* N and L increase without limit, the estimates for both sets of parameters are consistent.

The joint estimates of the artificial example are shown in Table 5.2a. Clearly, the uncorrected and corrected estimates are substantially different from each other, but the latter are very similar to the conditional estimates. The solution equations 5.9 are satisfied, of course, by the uncorrected estimates, and the $\hat{\pi}_{ri}$ shown in Table 5.2a are based on these uncorrected estimates.

To see how the solution equations 5.9a are satisfied, consider item 1. Substituting the $\hat{\pi}_{ri}$ values shows that $-s_1 + [n_1\hat{\pi}_{11} + n_2\hat{\pi}_{21}] = -7 + 5(0.545) + 5(0.855) = 0.00$.

Note that while the observed values for any person with a score r on each item is $x_{ri} = 0$ or $x_{ri} = 1$, the values $\hat{\pi}_{ri}$ lie *between* 0 and 1, that is, $0 < \hat{\pi}_{ri} < 1$. (Only for r = 0 or L does $\hat{\pi}_{ri} = 0$ or 1.) However, the probabilities $\hat{\pi}_{ri}$ are estimated so that their sum, $\Sigma_i\hat{\pi}_{ri}$, is equal to the sum $\Sigma_i x_{ri} = r$, that is, $r = \Sigma_i\hat{\pi}_{ri}$.

Standard errors. Approximate estimates of the standard errors of the estimates, $\hat{\sigma}_i$ and $\hat{\sigma}_r$, arise from the iterative estimation algorithm, and are obtained, respectively, from

$$\hat{\sigma}_i^2 = 1/\sum_{r=1}^{L-1} n_r \hat{\pi}_{ri}(1 - \hat{\pi}_{ri}) \qquad [5.10a]$$

and

$$\hat{\sigma}_r^2 = 1/\sum_{i=1}^{L} \hat{\pi}_{n}(1 - \hat{\pi}_{ri}) \qquad [5.10b]$$

It is evident that the structure of equation 5.10a is identical to that of equation 5.6, the approximation from the conditional estimates. Clearly, $\hat{\sigma}_r^2$ is the estimate of the variance of β_r, the location of a person with a score of r.

Example continued. Table 5.1 shows that the conditional and joint (corrected) estimates of the item parameters for the ENS are extremely close to each other: No misinterpretation would result if the latter procedure were used.

We can now present the person location parameters, although it is stressed that with only six items, these are very imprecise and they are shown here only illustratively. Table 5.2 shows those obtained by using equation 5.9b, with the conditional and joint estimates of $\hat{\delta}_i$. Clearly, any minor differences among the $\hat{\delta}_i$ produce an even more negligible effect on the estimates $\hat{\beta}_r$. This is a general property of the model.

TABLE 5.2a
Artificial Example of 10 Persons Responding to 3 Items
Joint Estimates of δ_i and β_r

		Estimates of δ_i	
i	Joint Uncorrected $\hat{\delta}_i$	Joint Corrected (δ_i^c)	Conditional
1	−0.978	−0.652	−0.640
2	0.000	0.000	0.000
3	0.978	0.652	0.640

$$\hat{\delta}_i^c = \hat{\delta}_i (L - 1)/L$$

$\hat{\pi}_{ri}$	1	2	3	n_r	$\hat{\beta}_r$
r 1	0.545	0.310	0.145	5	−0.798
2	0.855	0.690	0.455	5	0.798
s_i	7	5	3		

The relationship between r and $\hat{\beta}_r$ is displayed in Figure 5.2, showing that the total scores r are *linearized* into $\hat{\beta}_r$ with $\beta_0 = -\infty$ and $\beta_L = +\infty$.

Notice in Table 5.2 that the $\hat{\sigma}_r$ vary with r: As the denominator $\Sigma_i \hat{\pi}_{ri}(1 - \hat{\pi}_{ri})$ of equation 5.10b *increases, the standard error $\hat{\sigma}_r$ decreases.* The greatest contribution to the denominator from an item occurs when $\hat{\pi}_{ri}$ is the maximum, 0.5—that is, when $\hat{\beta}_r = \hat{\delta}_i$, and the contribution decreases as $|\hat{\beta}_r - \hat{\delta}_i|$ increases. Generally, the differences $|\hat{\beta}_r - \delta_i|$ are smaller for central values of r than for the extreme values. At the extremes, r = 0 and r = L, $\hat{\sigma}_r$ is infinite because $\hat{\pi}_{0i} = 0$ and $\hat{\pi}_{Li} = 1.0$, respectively, for all i. Because a large $|\beta_n - \delta_i|$ contributes very little to the precise location of person n, the items need to be targeted at the location of a person. This is consistent with our analogies with physical variables. Thus certain materials are useful for measuring temperatures within particular ranges, but they do not function as required and cease to provide information at extremes in either direction. It is possible to assign a finite value to extreme scores by extrapolation if one wishes to use the estimates of groups of individuals to compare, for example, their means. However, no amount of statistical finessing overcomes the lack of information for $\hat{\beta}_n$ at the extreme scores from person n's responses.

Pair-wise estimation. The pair-wise algorithm, employed consistently by Choppin (1968, 1983), involves taking the responses of each person to each pair of items and using the relationship of equation 3.11, from which we can write

TABLE 5.2
Person Location Estimates for Each Total Score
Using Both Conditional and Joint Item Parameter
Estimates for the ENS

Raw Score	From Conditional Item Estimates		From Joint Item Estimates	
r	$\hat{\beta}_r$	$\hat{\sigma}_r$	$\hat{\beta}_r$	$\hat{\sigma}_r$
0	$-\infty$	∞	$-\infty$	∞
1	-1.85	1.15	-1.85	1.15
2	-0.81	0.93	-0.81	0.94
3	0.00	0.87	0.00	0.89
4	0.81	0.93	0.82	0.93
5	1.84	1.14	1.85	1.15
6	∞	∞	∞	∞

$$\Pr\left\{(1,0);(\delta_i,\delta_j)\mid r=1\right\} = \frac{\exp(-\delta_i)}{\exp(-\delta_i)+\exp(-\delta_j)} = \pi_{ij} \qquad [5.11a]$$

and

$$\Pr\left\{(0,1);(\delta_i,\delta_j)\mid r=1\right\} = \frac{\exp(-\delta_j)}{\exp(-\delta_i)+\exp(-\delta_j)} = \pi_{ji} \qquad [5.11b]$$

To apply equation 5.11, the responses are rearranged into a pair comparison table, as in Table 5.3. For each pair of items (i, j), the number of persons F_{ij} who responded positively to one and negatively to the other, and the number f_{ij} who responded positively to i and f_{ji} who responded positively to j, can be obtained with $f_{ij} + f_{ji} = F_{ij}$.

For the pair of items (i, j), the probability of f_{ij} out of F_{ij} is given by the binomial distribution, namely,

$$\Pr\left\{(f_{ij},f_{ji});(\delta_i,\delta_j)\mid r=1\right\} = \frac{F_{ij}!\,\exp(-\delta_i)^{f_{ij}}\exp(-\delta_j)^{f_{ji}}}{f_{ij}!\,f_{ji}!\,[\exp(-\delta_i)+\exp(-\delta_j)]^{F_{ij}}}$$

The probability of the entire pair-wise frequency matrix is given by

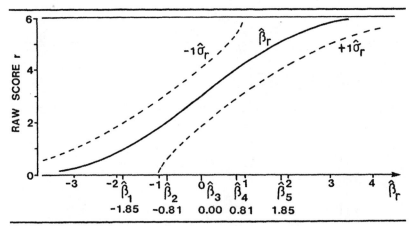

Figure 5.2: The Relationship Between Raw Scores r, Standard Errors $\hat{\sigma}_r$, and Estimates $\hat{\beta}_r$

$$\Lambda = \left(\prod_{\substack{i \ j \\ i \neq j}} \prod \frac{F_{ij}!}{f_{ij}! \, f_{ji}!} \right) \frac{\exp(-\sum_i \sum_j \delta_i f_{ij}) \exp(-\sum_i \sum_j \delta_j f_{ji})}{\prod_i \prod_j [\exp(-\delta_i) + \exp(-\delta_j)]^{F_{ij}}}$$

The logarithm of this likelihood, with C being a constant independent of the parameters, is

$$\log \Lambda = C - \sum_i \sum_j f_{ij} \delta_i - \sum_i \sum_j f_{ji} \delta_j - \sum_i \sum_j [\log \exp(-\delta_i) + \exp(-\delta_j)] , \; i \neq j,$$

and the solution equation, after differentiating $\log \Lambda$ and setting it equal to 0, is

$$-s_i + \sum_j F_{ij} \hat{\pi}_{ij} = 0, \qquad i = 1 \ldots L, \qquad [5.12]$$

where $s_i = \Sigma_j f_{ij}$ is the total number of times that item i is responded to positively and all other items are responded to negatively. Again, a constraint such as $\Sigma_i \hat{\delta}_i = 0.0$ must be imposed.

In the construction of the frequencies for a pair of items, the responses that are identical (either both 0 or both 1), are ignored. Therefore, the F_{ij} will vary across pairs of items. This feature can be exploited when not all persons respond to all items, as may occur when linking of items

TABLE 5.3
Constructed Pair-Wise Table

f_{ij}	1	2	3	•••	j	•••	L	$s_i = \sum_j f_{ij}$
				Items				
1	f_{11}	f_{12}	f_{13}	•••	f_{1j}	•••	f_{1L}	s_1
2	f_{21}	f_{22}	f_{23}	•••	f_{2j}	•••	f_{2L}	s_2
3	f_{31}	f_{32}	f_{33}	•••	f_{3j}	•••	f_{3L}	s_3
Items								
•	•	•	•	•	•	•		•
•	•	•	•	•	•	•		•
•	•	•	•	•	•	•		•
i	f_{il}	f_{i2}	f_{i3}	•••	f_{ij}	•••	f_{iL}	s_i
•	•	•	•	•	•	•		•
•	•	•	•	•	•	•	•	•
•	•	•	•	•	•	•		•
L	f_{L1}	f_{L2}	f_{L3}	•••	f_{Lj}	•••	f_{LL}	s_L

TABLE 5.3a
Constructed Pair-Wise Table for the Artificial Example of
10 Persons Responding to 3 Items Together with the
Pair-Wise Estimates

	f_{ij} (F_{ij})	1	2	3	$s_i = \sum_j f_{ij}$
			Items (j)		
	1		5(8)	5(6)	10
Items (i)	2	3(8)		4(6)	7
	3	1(6)	2(6)		3
	$\hat{\pi}_{ij}$	1	2	3	
	1		0.646	0.806	
Items (i)	2	0.354		0.694	
	3	0.194	0.306		
	$\hat{\delta}_i$	−0.674	−0.073	0.747	

$$-s_i + \sum_j F_{ij}\,\hat{\pi}_{ij} = 0,\ \hat{\pi}_{ij} = \exp(-\hat{\delta}_i) / (\exp.-\hat{\delta}_i) + \exp(-\hat{\delta}_j))$$

across a wide range of the continuum is required and it is not appropriate that all persons respond to all items. An example of linking is shown at the end of this chapter.

The pair-wise procedure involves a conceptual approximation of ML theory. This approximation results from treating the f_{ij} as independent when in reality they are dependent because overlapping persons are involved in each pair of items. Nevertheless, the resultant estimates seem excellent. Although the estimates are excellent, standard errors of the estimates and tests of fit between the data and the model cannot be made routinely using the pair-wise arrangement of the data. In the estimates of the standard errors that follow, equation 5.10a was used after the $\hat{\delta}_i$ were estimated by the pair-wise method and the $\hat{\beta}_r$ and $\hat{\sigma}_r$ were estimated respectively by equations 5.9b and 5.10b of the joint method.

The construction of the frequency matrix f_{ij}, the pair-wise estimates for the artificial example, together with the reconstructed $\hat{\pi}_{ij}$, are shown in Table 5.3a. The solution equation for item 1, for example, is satisfied according to

$$-s_1 + F_{11}\hat{\pi}_{11} + F_{12}\hat{\pi}_{12} = 0, \text{ that is, } -10 + 8\,(0.646) + 6\,(0.806) = 0.00$$

Example continued. Table 5.1 includes the estimates of the ENS example from the pair-wise method. It is evident that the estimates obtained by all three methods effectively are the same.

Linking. The pair-wise procedure leads into the topic of linking or chaining of test items, an issue that has become important in educational and psychological testing. Linking is concerned with the placing of items of a certain class on the same scale or metric, even if it is not possible, or desirable, for every person for whom the items are relevant to respond to all of the items. Indeed, such a situation faced Rasch (1960/1980) when he first tackled the problem of studying the improvement in reading ability of children following special reading instruction: At an early stage, children were given relatively easy words and at later stages they were given progressively more and more difficult (and therefore different) words, and yet the task was to quantify the improvement in reading ability.

It was from this practical task that Rasch required a calibration of the reading texts to be independent of the individuals (from a specified class) used to collect the data, and that the subsequent measurement of the individual be independent of the particular reading text administered.

Such requirements continue to be common in educational and psychological testing, both in studying change and in studying distributions of abilities. Thus, if a set of items is appropriate for a person at the beginning of a program of study, say, it will most likely be too easy at the end of it. Similarly, when a specified and identical set of items must be administered to persons with a wide range of abilities, items that are appropriate for the less able will be too easy for the more able, and vice versa. Effects of this kind at the extremes of tests are known as *floor and ceiling effects*.

To overcome floor and ceiling effects, adaptive testing procedures, in which each person answers questions that are moderately difficult for him or her, are becoming more popular, especially with the advent of computer-adaptive testing (CAT). The principle in CAT is that if an item is answered correctly, the next item chosen is more difficult, and if it is answered incorrectly, the next item chosen is easier. Such a principle in the choice of items is known as *tailored testing*.

A second problem with repeated testing is the familiarity of the persons with the specific items. A similar problem can be particularly relevant in attitude and personality testing. The construction and scaling of items that are on the same metric makes many parallel tests available in the sense that the location estimate of a person should be independent of the specific items used to compose a test.

Wright and Stone (1979) describe approaches to linking, and to testing the quality of the links, with the SLM. The pair-wise estimation procedure makes the linking routine if there are enough persons who overlap in their responses to the items. Of course, overlapping response matrices are required for all linking procedures.

An example of such linking is shown below. The two sets of items linked come from the well-known nonverbal psychological test of Raven's Progressive Matrices (ACER, 1958; Raven et al., 1938). The different versions of this test include the Standard Progressive Matrices (SPM) containing 60 items and the Advanced Progressive Matrices (APM) containing 36 items. Even though the items in the two sets are based on similar principles, traditionally they are administered as separate complete sets.

In a recent study (Andrich, 1986), the SPM and APM items were amalgamated and administered with the aid of a computer according to tailored testing principles. For illustrative purposes, Table 5.4 shows a portion of the person-by-item response matrix to 11 items of the SPM and 9 items of the APM. As can be seen, different persons encountered different items. Table 5.5 shows a portion of the reconstructed pair-wise

TABLE 5.4

Responses of Selected Persons to 20 Items of the PRM:
Items are in Order of Their Difficulty and
Persons are in Order of Their Ability

Person	Ability	St. Error	Fit Index	Response Pattern
6	−1.78	0.60	−.245	1 00 00 0 0
20	−1.32	0.56	−.063	0 1 00 0
30	−1.11	0.54	−.097	0 1 0 00
38	−0.99	0.54	4.284	11 0000 0100001 10
48	−0.91	0.53	−.552	1110 1 01 000 0000
52	−0.78	0.53	−.429	11100 1 10 0100 0000
62	−0.40	0.52	−.276	111010 10 1010 0 00
63	−0.40	0.52	2.929	1 10 01 00 10 0001
68	−0.32	0.52	−.111	01 1 00 0
74	−0.14	0.53	−.762	1111 10110 100 0000
80	−0.05	0.53	.473	1101 1 1001 0 100
87	0.07	0.53	−.895	1111 11110 0 0 0 00
95	0.28	0.54	−.292	1 1 001 0
101	0.52	0.55	−.985	111111 111 00 0 00
115	0.88	0.57	−.859	111 1 11 101 0000
122	1.09	0.59	1.218	1 11 1 10 01 00011
129	1.30	0.62	2.680	011 11 111 1 1 00
136	1.57	0.63	−.057	111 1 10 1111 00
144	1.87	0.67	−.491	1111 11 11 1 01 0
151	2.92	0.82	−.148	1111 11 11 1 01 1

table, as well as the item difficulty (parameter) estimates. Table 5.4 also shows the ability (parameter) estimates of the persons, where the β_r were obtained using equation 5.9b separately for each individual and with the $\hat{\delta}_i$ shown in Table 5.5. It also shows the estimated standard error of $\hat{\beta}_r$ and a fit statistic Y_n which is explained in the next chapter. (Figure 5.3 shows the items on the same scale and includes the distribution of persons.) Nothing special needed to be done to effect the linking using the pair-wise estimation procedure.[2]

The 11 items of the SPM were from the 12 items of Set E, the most difficult set from the SPM, and the 9 items from the APM were from the 12 items of Set A, the easiest from the APM. (In each case one item was used as a practice item and two others from the APM were used too infrequently for estimation to be effective.) Because the two versions of the test overlap considerably, it is not surprising that the easiest items from the APM are easier than the hardest items from the SPM, as revealed in the estimates of item difficulties and shown in Figure 5.3.

TABLE 5.5
Reconstructed Pair-Wise Table for 20 Items of the
Raven's Progressive Matrices, and Item Parameter Estimates

F_{ij}	f_{ij}	S_1	S_2	S_3	S_4	•••	A_8	A_9	A_{10}	$\hat{\delta}_i$
					Items					
	S1	—	41	8	20	•••	6	7	5	0.137
	S2	3	—	11	12	•••	1	6	3	−0.899
	S3	27	5	—	15	•••	2	5	5	0.447
	S4	12	25	1	—	•••	4	3	4	−0.395
	S5	25	45	20	13	•••	8	11	6	0.429
	S6	28	49	15	30	•••	4	6	3	2.330
	S7	34	51	23	34	•••	17	18	16	2.719
	S8	15	17	8	11	•••	2	3	3	−0.495
	S9	12	16	7	12	•••	3	1	3	1.146
	S10	10	17	10	13	•••	9	14	9	1.551
	S11	11	20	12	16	•••	10	18	11	2.918
	A1	2	2	0	2	•••	0	3	0	−2.226
	A2	0	3	0	3	•••	1	3	1	−1.414
	A3	0	2	0	2	•••	1	3	1	−0.362
	A4	0	2	0	2	•••	0	2	0	−2.260
	A5	0	3	1	1	•••	1	4	1	−0.655
	A6	1	6	1	5	•••	2	4	5	−0.034
	A7	1	1	0	0	•••	—	2	1	−1.077
	A8	2	2	0	3	•••	1	—	5	−1.057
	A9	1	2	1	1	•••	3	1	—	−0.804

NOTE: S = standard; A = advanced.

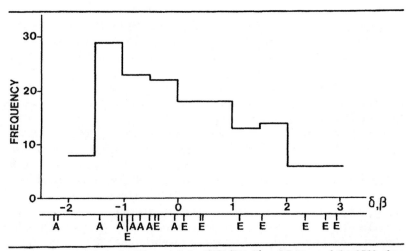

Figure 5.3: Location of 11 Items of the SPM (Set E) and 9 Items of the APM when Linked, and the Frequency Distribution of the Sample

Conclusion

We have now covered the main features of the methods of estimation, and illustrated their application. It may appear surprising that such a simple model can generate as much research and literature on estimation as it has done. Tests of fit between the data and the model are beginning to generate even more. This body of literature seems to arise in part from the model itself. Thus, while the model appears simple, this simplicity is deceptive, and on further reflection, the model has extensive and subtle consequences. These consequences fascinate many researchers. Their fascination is related to the structural invariance of comparisons and to the feeling that the model reflects something fundamental or basic in quantitative research in social science. While many different models may account for any given set of dichotomously scored data, the SLM has a basis independent of any data. We turn to the tests of fit between the model and the data in the next chapter.

6. TESTS OF FIT: ACCORD BETWEEN THE MODEL AND THE DATA

This chapter studies some methods of checking the accord between the model and the data. The topic was broached when we studied the differences between the ratios of responses for a pair of items across total scores. Before embarking on further specific techniques, some general points are noted. First, it is standard practice in statistical modeling to compare how well different models account for the data. Generally, the orientation is to consider the data as fixed and to choose the model that best fits the data. Such a perspective arises in part because statistical analysis comes after the data are collected and it is often carried out by statisticians or methodologists rather than by the researcher who collected the data on the basis of some theoretical position.

A different relationship between the model and the data—one in which they have a more symmetrical role—is taken here. Thus, if there is discord between the data and a model, it is left an open question whether the model or the data are at fault (Rasch, 1960/1980). It is conceivable that when the data do not accord with the model with which they are intended to accord, that something has gone astray with the data or its collection. It is possible that modifying some aspects of the data collection, or reinterpreting or modifying the frame of reference, may produce a more convincing interpretation than does a change of the model.

Second, the smaller the number of parameters, the less likely the model will accord with the data. Usually, those parameters should account for the most salient features of the data and be the most stable across replications. Third, because no model is perfect (it being some kind of summary of the data), the chance a model will fit varies inversely with the precision of the estimates. Therefore, the poorer the precision, the more likely data will fit the model. Furthermore, the precision of the estimates of parameters depends upon the sample size—the larger the sample size, the greater the precision. Thus the larger the sample, the less likely the data will show fit to the model.

This fit relationship between the data and the model is true of any modeling, deterministic and statistical, quantitative and nonquantitative. Ultimately, whether the fit can be considered good enough must come from outside the data and is relative to the precision deemed necessary in the field of inquiry (Kuhn, 1961). Unfortunately, most statistical tests of fit are internal to the data. As a result, they can give misleading substantive impressions—either that the model is not adequate for its purpose when it is, or the other way around.

The above points are general, but there are some further, more specific points in the concern about the SLM. In applying the SLM, one is not simply modeling data, one is checking the degree to which a variable with properties of fundamental measurement has been constructed. Part of the trade-off in constructing fundamental measures is that the SLM has a minimum number of parameters and will therefore generally be violated more readily than models with more parameters.

Checking the data. That the data may be at fault in some sense is not a foreign idea in test and questionnaire construction. When a scale is to be constructed, many more items than make up the final scale are trialed. In general, all of the original items have face or content validity according to experts' understandings of the construct. Statistical criteria are employed to check the consistency and empirical validity of the responses to the items. These criteria may vary among approaches, but generally, they are aimed at constructing a scale that will achieve the most precise measurements. Most importantly, the analysis of the data can point to those responses that are inconsistent.

It is customary to modify some items on the basis of the data. However, the items should not simply be discarded—they should be studied and hypotheses generated to explain why they do not accord with the model, as do the other items. Discarding items simply on statistical criteria creates risks of capitalizing on sampling errors of various kinds and thereby reduces the chances of a general application of the test. Thus, while items may be discarded as identities, the empirical information they provide should be incorporated into the construction and modification of other items and the understanding of the variable.

In the measurement of attitude, Thurstone expected to review the relevant literature in a field and to generate some 100 statements in order to retain 20 or 30 on the basis of the statistical criteria. The ENS scale has also been modified on the basis of the statistical criteria: Items were selected in order to make the correlation between a scale of Extroversion and Neuroticism "disappear" (Eysenck and Eysenck, 1964). This further justifies considering both the data and the model, not simply the model. Unfortunately, space does not permit exploring the theory behind the ENS data in detail. With the above points clarified, we will use the conventional terminology for convenience and refer to "test of fit" between the model and the data.

Fit Tests with Respect to the Total Score: Check on the ICCs

There are two principal approaches in conducting statistical fit tests with the SLM. The first involves estimating the model parameters from the entire data set and then checking how well various partitions of the data can be recovered from the model and the parameter estimates. The second invokes the condition that the parameter estimates should be invariant across different partitions of the data, and involves comparing parameter estimates from such partitions. Both of course, study consequences of the model in relation to the observed data. Both are illustrated now with the ENS example.

Comparing observed and model proportions and frequencies. First note equation B.2 from Appendix B.

$$\hat{\pi}_{ri} = \Pr\{x_{ni} = 1 \mid r_n\} = \exp(-\hat{\delta}_i)\hat{\gamma}_{r-1,i}/\hat{\gamma}_r \qquad [6.1]$$

Inserting the estimates $(-\hat{\delta}_i)$ in equation 6.1 gives the probability estimates $\hat{\pi}_{ri}$ that persons with a score of r obtain 1 on item i. These are shown in Table 6.1. π_{ri} was also estimated in the joint estimation procedure. Inserting estimates $\hat{\beta}_r$ and $\hat{\delta}_i$ in equation 5.8c gives

$$\hat{\pi}_{ri} = \exp(\hat{\beta}_r - \hat{\delta}_i)/(1 + \exp(\hat{\beta}_r - \hat{\delta}_i)) \qquad [6.2]$$

Estimates from equation 6.2 are carried through in parallel with those of equation 6.1. Both are shown in Table 6.1 and it is evident that they are very similar. These estimates are now compared with the observed proportions from Table 2.2, and repeated in Table 6.1.

Comparisons between the estimated probabilities and the observed proportions can be formalized as follows: The statistic

$$\chi^2 = \sum_r^{L-1} \sum_i^{L} (n_n - n_r \hat{\pi}_{ri})^2 / [n_n \hat{\pi}_{ri}(1 - \hat{\pi}_{ri})] \qquad [6.3]$$

is distributed as χ^2 on $(L-1)(L-2)$ degrees of freedom (df). These values are shown in Table 6.1. Wright and Panchapakesan (1969) originally proposed this statistic based on the joint estimation procedure. Van den Wollenberg (1982) studied these statistics and concluded that the one based on the joint estimates was inadequate. However, care must be taken to use the *uncorrected* item parameter estimates and the corresponding ability estimates because it is these that satisfy the equalities between the observed and the expected marginals s_i and r_n.

In addition, because the distributions are asymptotically χ^2, and because $\hat{\delta}_i$ and $\hat{\beta}_n$ are consistent as *both* N and L increase, the Wright and Panchapakesan statistic is appropriate. The case here has only six items, yet the two sets of recovered probabilities are almost identical.

With many more items and moderate sample sizes, it is not unusual to have total score groups with small frequencies. G-class intervals may be formed from adjacent score groups and then the statistic is distributed on $(G-1)(L-1)$ df. Further details and refinements on these statistics may be found in Gustafsson (1980b), Molenaar (1963), and Van den Wollenberg (1982). It is clear that according to either method of calculating the χ^2 statistics, the data and the model of the ENS example do not accord.

One reason that the misfit is so great is the large sample size—with such a large sample the parameters are estimated with great precision and any misfit is readily exposed. This does not mean that the model is not useful in capturing some of the essentials of the data. An idea of how

TABLE 6.1
Probabilities and Proportions for Persons with a Total Score r
Who Respond Positively to Item i

Raw Score r			Items 1	2	3	4	5	6	n_r
1	(1)	π	.38	.10	.03	.11	.06	.31	
	(2)	π	.37	.11	.03	.12	.06	.32	318
	(3)	p	.35	.04	.04	.16	.05	.36	
2	(1)	π	.65	.25	.09	.27	.15	.59	
	(2)	π	.64	.26	.08	.28	.15	.58	352
	(3)	p	.66	.18	.05	.32	.21	.59	
3	(1)	π	.81	.46	.18	.49	.29	.77	
	(2)	π	.81	.46	.18	.48	.30	.77	298
	(3)	p	.78	.47	.14	.45	.40	.77	
4	(1)	π	.90	.68	.33	.70	.50	.88	
	(2)[i]	π	.91	.67	.34	.69	.51	.89	295
	(3)	p	.94	.76	.38	.64	.42	.86	
5	(1)	π	.96	.87	.58	.88	.76	.96	
	(2)	π	.97	.86	.60	.87	.75	.96	219
	(3)	p	.97	.95	.63	.87	.64	.94	
Total			.72	.44	.22	.46	.32	.68	1482

(1) conditional $\hat{\pi}_{ri}$ $\quad : \hat{\pi}_{ri} = \Pr\{x_{ni} = 1 \mid r\} = \exp(-\delta_i)\,\gamma_{r-1,i}/\gamma_r$

(2) joint (uncorrected) $\hat{\pi}_{ri}$ $\quad : \hat{\pi}_{ri} = \exp(\hat{\beta}_r - \hat{\delta}_i)/(1 + \exp(\hat{\beta}_r - \hat{\delta}_i))$

(3) observed p_{ri} $\quad : p_{ri} = f_{ri}/n_r$

$\quad x^2{}_{(1)} = 147.30 \qquad df = 20, p < 0.001 \quad$ (from conditional π_{ri})

$\quad x^2{}_{(2)} = 143.29 \qquad df = 20, p < .001 \quad$ (from joint π_{ri})

$\quad x^2_L \quad = 132.25 \qquad df = 20, p < .001 \quad$ (likelihood ratio test)

good it is in doing so may be seen graphically. A graphical display can also show where any misfit is most pronounced.

Graphical representation: The ICC. Figure 6.1 displays the $\hat{\pi}_{ri}$ based on the conditional item scale estimates ($\hat{\delta}_i$) for items 1, 2, and 5, together with the observed proportions. Note that the scale of the abscissa now, unlike in Figure 2.1, is that of the $\hat{\beta}_r$ values, rather than the raw scores r, because the $\hat{\beta}_r$ are on a linearized scale.

66

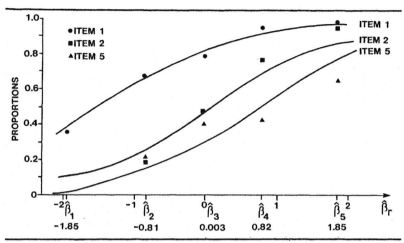

Figure 6.1: Theoretical Proportions Based on Conditional Estimates, and Observed Proportions for 3 Items

While the statistical tests used earlier suggest gross misfit between the data and the model, the graphs indicate general consistency. In addition, the graphs reveal the directions of the misfit. Specifically, item 1 shows no systematic violation of the model, while items 2 and 5 show two distinct trends of particular interest. First, item 5 does not discriminate as expected—the rate of change of the proportions as a function of the location is less than expected. But, because the simultaneous scaling of the persons and the items makes the slope of the model curves an average (geometric mean) of the slopes of all items, this implies that item 5 does not discriminate as well as this average. In contrast, item 2 discriminates more sharply than this average.

It may be suggested that item 5 (low discrimination) captures some trait different from that of the other items—it tends to violate unidimensionality with respect to the other items. On the other hand, item 2 (high discrimination) is overly dependent on the other items. That is, if one tends to agree (disagree) with the other items, then one is even more likely to agree (disagree) with item 2 than would be expected from the average agreement (disagreement) with the items. Thus the requirement of independence seems to be violated by this item.

These interpretations for the ICCs of items 5 and 2 imply that they show different kinds of misfit. Each, however, manifests that both independence and unidimensionality have been violated; it is simply a question of emphasis. One can contrive misfit of both kinds just by introducing extra parameters in the responses or just by violating the condition of independence (Andrich, 1985).

It is opportune to mention here the two-parameter model (so called because it has two item parameters) that takes the form

$$\Pr\{x_{ni} = 1 \; ; \; \beta_n, \delta i \; \alpha_i\} = \exp(\alpha_i(\beta_n - \delta_i))/\gamma_{ni} \qquad [6.4]$$

where $\gamma_{ni} = 1 + \exp(\alpha_i(\beta_n - \delta_i))$ (Birnbaum, 1968). The α_i in this expression attempts to capture the differences in discriminations of the ICCs. The model destroys the possibility of explicit invariance of the estimates of the person and the item parameters and will, therefore, not be pursued here. The model, has, however, generated a great deal of literature and debate in educational and psychological measurement (*Journal of Educational Measurement*, 1977, Vol. 14, No. 2; Hambleton, 1983; Hulin et al., 1983; Wright, 1977, 1984).

Graphical representation: simultaneous linearization. Graphs that bring out the simultaneous linearization $\lambda_{ni} = \beta_n - \delta_i$ may be drawn. Rasch (1960) used such graphs in his checks between model and data. Using the conditional estimates ($\hat{\delta}_i$), the linear relationship $\log(\hat{\pi}_{ri}/(1 - \hat{\pi}_{ri})) = \hat{\lambda}_{ri} = \hat{\beta}_r - \hat{\delta}_i$ can be formed and compared with the observed values $l_{ri} = \log(p_{ri}/(1 - p_{ri}))$. Figure 6.2 shows these graphs. The linear plots show the same information as the ICC plots, although the linear metric lends itself more readily to the study of residuals (Mead, 1976; Wright and Stone, 1979). These will be considered when the fit of persons is studied, but the parallel lines for the (modeled) estimates do show that, according to the model, the difference between the scale values of any two items is invariant across the continuum.

Likelihood ratio tests. A test based explicitly on the hypothesis that the conditional item parameter estimates should be independent of the locations of the persons has also been devised (Andersen, 1973b). Item parameter estimates are calculated for the group as a whole and then recalculated for persons in each group r. If $L(\hat{\delta}_i)$ is the conditional likelihood (i.e., the probability of the observations with the estimated

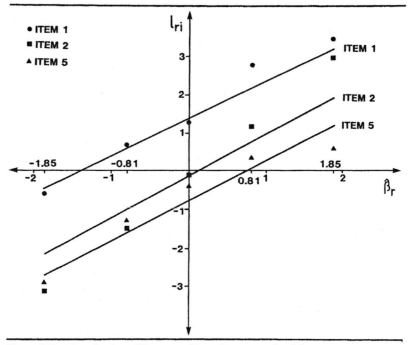

Figure 6.2: Linearization of Person and Item Parameters for 3 Items

parameters) and $L(\hat{\delta}_i^{(r)})$ is the same likelihood but with estimates based only on persons with a score of r, then $-2\log[L(\hat{\delta}_i)/\Pi_r L(\hat{\delta}_i^{(r)})]$ is also distributed as χ^2 on $(L - 1)(L - 2)$ df. Again, when sample sizes in the score groups are small, adjacent class intervals may be formed, and, if there are G-class intervals, then the df are $(G - 1)(L - 1)$. For our example, this statistic is shown as χ_L^2 in Table 6.1 and has the value 132.25 on 20 df.

Each of the above checks on the model involves subdividing the data into class intervals according to the total scores. In so doing, the check is primarily on the stability of the ICC across the continuum. That is, the check is centered on the question of whether or not a joint or simultaneous transformation can be made on the persons and the items so that an additive structure results.

While this general approach is straightforward, for a given sample size more powerful tests can be constructed when specific hypotheses for model violation are put to the test (see Gustafsson, 1980a, 1980b). We will see this effect in the remainder of the chapter.

Reproduction of the Guttman pattern. In Chapter 4, we showed that given a total score r, each pattern has an explicit model probability of being observed, with the Guttman pattern having the greatest probability. While all patterns could be reproduced, together with the observed and estimated frequencies (see Kelderman, 1984), for simplicity Table 6.2 shows only the Guttman pattern and its observed and estimated frequency. According to this criterion, the data fit the Guttman structure very well. However, we have ignored any violations of the Rasch model among the patterns other than the Guttman pattern, and therefore this test is not as sensitive as it might be.

Invariance of Parameter Estimates
Across Designated Classes

The principle of invariance can be invoked across classifications other than class intervals. Indeed, it is though a checking of the invariance across persons and items that the frame of reference can be extended or constrained. Thus classes of persons can be formed according to age, socioeconomic status, and so on. The choice of classification rests on the theoretical or a priori considerations relevant to the construction of the variable. Classifications of persons should be made on those features that are relevant to the case and that are the most likely to show a breakdown of the model.

Two preliminary points are noted before the ENS data are partitioned according to sex. First, if the scale values of the items show invariance across sexes, then the scale can be used to investigate *differences in degree*: The means of the males and females can be compared. On the other hand, if such invariance is not evident, then the difference between the sexes is a *difference in kind*. It becomes, then, a question of understanding and interpreting the nature of the difference and the criterion of fundamental measurement is used to help explore the data with a view to understanding any underlying processes that distinguish the two. Of course, it must be kept in mind that identifying a difference in kind is also a relative matter—with a large enough sample, one can always be found.

Second, specific objectivity, in Rasch's terms, has given rise to expressions such as "sample-free" or "population-free." This terminology can be confusing because of the two senses in which "sample" and

TABLE 6.2
Observed and Estimated Frequencies of Each Guttman Pattern,
Conditional on the Total Score

Pattern (Items)[a]						Probabilities		Frequencies	
1	6	4	2	5	3	Observed	Estimated	Observed	Estimated
0	0	0	0	0	0	1.000	1.000	308	308
1	0	0	0	0	0	0.352	0.378	112	120.204
1	1	0	0	0	0	0.369	0.326	130	114.752
1	1	1	0	0	0	0.174	0.218	52	64.964
1	1	1	1	0	0	0.275	0.275	81	81.125
1	1	1	1	1	0	0.365	0.417	80	91.323
1	1	1	1	1	1	1.000	1.000	177	177

NOTE: $\chi^2 = 8.703$; df = 5; p > 0.10.

"population" are used in statistics: One sense denotes an empirical class of entities, in this case males or females; the other concerns theoretical distributional properties under sampling. With these distinctions, it is stressed that the SLM provides item scale estimates that are free of the *distribution* of locations of persons—providing the model holds. As noted earlier, whether the model holds across different classes of persons is an empirical question: The model is an expression of an intention that it does hold across the classes.

Male and female scale values. Table 6.3 shows the scale values for males and females, together with their standard errors. A statistical index for each item can be constructed according to

$$Z_i = (\hat{\delta}_{i(M)} - \hat{\delta}_{i(F)})/[\hat{\sigma}^2_{i(M)} + \hat{\sigma}^2_{i(F)}]^{1/2} \qquad [6.5]$$

With large sample sizes, Z_i approximates a random normal deviate. Then an overall statistic $\chi^2_Z = \Sigma_i Z_i^2$ can be formed and checked against a χ^2 distribution on L – 1 df, though it is not distributed exactly as χ^2 (Van den Wollenberg, 1982). The value of this index, χ^2_Z, is also shown in Table 6.3. The statistic is particularly useful in detecting differences in scale values between groups for specific items and can be generalized readily to include more classifications, including those that may form one-way and two-way tables (Andrich and Kline, 1981).

This same information can be captured graphically. The null hypothesis line of no difference between $\hat{\delta}_{i(M)}$ and $\hat{\delta}_{i(F)}$ is a straight line of unit slope, and confidence bands corresponding to standard errors can be

TABLE 6.3
Scale Values of Items of the ENS for Males and Females

Item	Scale Values and (Standard Errors)				Squared Standardized Difference Z_i^2
	M		F		
1	−.89	(.09)	−1.47	(.09)	20.96
6	−.85	(.09)	−1.12	(.09)	4.47
4	.07	(.09)	.03	(.09)	.07
2	.16	(.08)	.11	(.09)	0.15
5	.40	(.09)	1.04	(.09)	25.48
3	1.12	(.09)	1.41	(1.00)	4.71

$\chi^2_Z = 55.85$; df = 5; p << .01
$\chi^2_L = 98.00$; df = 5; p << .01

$\sum_i Z_i^2 = 55.85$

formed. These are shown in Figure 6.3. It can be seen from this figure that item 5 violates the model most. The males endorse it relatively more than the females. This is one of the two items detected as misfitting substantially according to the ICC curves—namely, the one with a discrimination lower than the average. However, item 2, which showed a greater discrimination than the average, shows very similar scale values for males and females. These two items illustrate that different methods of checking the model emphasize (and, therefore, can detect more readily) different kinds of misfit.

Of course, the likelihood ratio test

$$\chi^2_L = -2\log[L(\hat{\delta}_i) / L(\hat{\delta}_i)^{(M)} L(\hat{\delta}_i)^{(F)}] \qquad [6.6]$$

used earlier with score groups can be constructed on the male-female classification. This value is also shown in Table 6.3 as χ^2_L. The values of both χ^2_Z and χ^2_L show misfit. (The difference between the two values could be caused by doing the calculations for the first statistic from the output showing only three decimal places. The rounding effects with small likelihood values and small standard scores could have created the large discrepancy.)

In addition to breaking down the data according to an external criterion, such as we have done, it is possible to classify groups on the basis of the responses to some specific item (Molenaar, 1983). The same

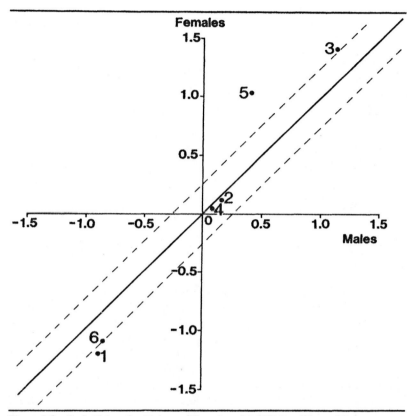

Figure 6.3   Scale Values for Males and Females with 95% Confidence Limits

techniques are applicable, with the interpretation then being in relation to the item rather than the a priori classification.

In educational tests of attainment, items that scale differently in different groups are said to be *biased*. This term is used because some items are relatively more difficult for some groups than for other groups—as item 5 is with respect to males and females. It should be stressed that only a *relative* bias of items within a test can be detected by such methods, on the assumption that the test as a whole is less biased than any particular item.

A comparison of a pair of items across sexes. More elaborate tests of fit that incorporate the invariance across both the total score groups and across different classes of persons can be constructed. With very small numbers of items, say three or four, the analysis can be cast into the form of log-linear models (Kelderman, 1984; Duncan, 1984). We will not deal with this approach formally here as it requires knowledge of the log-linear model literature (Knoke and Burke, 1980; Bishop et al., 1975). Instead, we will consider an orientation to such an extension by studying the responses of just items 2 and 4 more closely. These two items are chosen because, on the whole, they show the greatest relative consistency across the sexes.

This consistency is observed from Table 6.3, but it can be confirmed readily by a χ^2 statistic as in the top *left* part of Table 6.4. The top left part of this table shows, for each sex, the odds of a positive response to one item rather than the other, when only one of the items has a positive response. The χ^2 value to its right shows that these two items have equivalent scale values across the sexes. The extremely good fit results because the items were chosen for their similar location values with respect to the sexes—they were not selected at random. Nevertheless, this pair is useful to make a point.

Table 6.4 shows the same data, but it is classified further according to total scores. Because the persons in the score groups are distinct persons, a standard χ^2 statistic can be calculated *within* each score group, and it, too, is distributed on a single df. These χ^2s may therefore be summed to give a χ^2 on 5 df. Again, the table shows that the relative ratios of the males and females are equivalent. With such equivalence evident, we may challenge the model even more by estimating a single relative parameter across the males and females for the odds of a positive endorsement to one of the items. This is given by $(170 + 175)/(156 + 162) = 1.085$. Using this ratio, the frequencies in each cell in the lower part of Table 6.4 can be estimated and a χ^2 statistic constructed. For example, the predicted values in the cells with observed frequencies 28 and 4 are 16.64 and 15.36, respectively.

Comparing this pair of observed and expected frequencies give a χ^2 value of 21.63. Summing over all 10 pairs of cells gives a χ^2 value of 58.82 on 9 df. This value is clearly significant at the 0.05 level, and even though some of the observed frequencies are small, no expected frequency is less than 5.

It can, therefore, be inferred that while the overall relative odds for the males and females are equivalent, and while they are equivalent within each score group, they are different from score group to score group. Thus, by breaking the data into more and more systematic classes, a particular kind of misfit has been disclosed. What is shown in

TABLE 6.4
Relative Odds of Endorsement Between Items 2 and 4
Classified by Sex

	Items		Sex			Expected Value Under
	2	4	M	F		the Single Ratio
	0	1	170	175	$x^2 = 0.01$ $df = 1$	$\dfrac{170 + 175}{156 + 162} = 1.085$
	1	0	156	162	$p > 0.05$	
r	2	4	M	F		M F
1	0	1	28	22	$x^2 = 1.98$	16.64 15.60
	1	0	4	8	$p > 0.05$	15.36 14.40
2	0	1	52	55	$x^2 = 2.45$	45.24 40.04
	1	0	35	22	$p > 0.05$	41.76 36.96
3	0	1	50	62	$x^2 = 0.37$	40.96 68.64
	1	0	48	70	$p > 0.05$	47.04 63.36
4	0	1	33	33	$x^2 = 0.02$	44.20 43.16
	1	0	52	50	$p > 0.05$	40.80 39.84
5	0	1	77	3	$x^2 = 0.41$	12.48 7.80
	1	0	17	12	$p > 0.05$	11.52 7.20
					$x^2 = 5.22$ $df = 5$ $p > 0.05$	$x^2 = 58.82$ $df = 9$ $p > 0.05$

Table 6.4 is that the *low scorers*, both male and female, endorse item 4 more readily than item 2 (if they endorse only one of the items), but in contrast, *high scorers* endorse item 2 more readily than item 4.

What should be done with such evidence? Ideally, one would select persons with the various response patterns to the two items, interview them, and try to understand how these two items produced the observed interaction across score groups that is invariant across sexes. Rather than trying to identify a more complicated model that might include the interaction, it is important to understand substantively why the two items operate inversely across persons more and less neurotic, as defined by the scale. At this point, a clinical psychologist or a sociologist (depending on the point of view taken) is required, not a psychometrician. However, armed with the goal of fundamental measurement, the psychometrician can identify the specific substantive questions that need to be answered. (By the way of an analogy, if one disclosed an anomaly in measurement in the physical sciences, such as the expansion of water in relation to mercury at $0°$ C, one would study the fluids more systematically and one would not use the expansion of water in this range to measure temperature.)

A systematic scale effect across sexes. One final examination of relative scale values is made now. We return to Table 6.3. Rather than displaying the relative difficulties in the conventional way as in Figure 6.3, to help stress an observation, they are graphed on parallel lines as in Figure 6.4. Now it is clear that while items 4 and 2 are, on the whole, relatively stable across the sexes (even though they are not stable across the raw scores), the scale is stretched much more for the females than the males. With such evidence it would be difficult to sustain a simple comparison of mean scores (a difference in degree) between the males and females—the scaling manifests a difference in kind, even though the items scale in the same order.

The items that the males tend not to endorse, the females tend to endorse even less, while items that the males tend to endorse, the females tend to endorse even more, in a relative sense. This can be seen from the odds ratios of the extreme items, items 1 and 3, shown in Table 6.5. It is clear that if a male and a female endorse one of items 1 and 3, then the odds that it is item 1 for the male (0.114) is greater than it is for the female (0.040). This difference in ratio is evidence by the χ^2 value of 13.74 on 1 df.

With such a systematic difference in scale, it may be tempting to make a linear transformation of the scale values of the items of either the males or females in order to equate them. While the location estimates of the person parameters associated with a given total score may then be more comparable statistically, it still leaves unanswered the more fundamental question as to whether they are comparable psychologically or sociologically.

It seems that at a relatively refined level of analysis we have uncovered a systematic difference in kind between the sexes, even though our aim was to confirm that the intended simple addition of the raw scores was justified. It may be useful at this point to note that had we not used a model that captured the intention of simple addition of the item responses, but had used the model of equation 6.4, which allowed for differences in item discriminations as a function of the raw scores, then the hypotheses of equal odds (of the endorsed versus the nonendorsed item pairs) across score groups and across sexes that we investigated would not have been generated. Instead, the differences in item discrimination would have absorbed some of the differences that were exposed

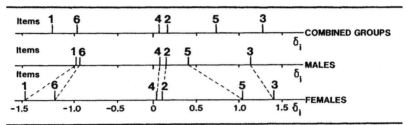

Figure 6.4: Relative Scale Values of Males, Females, and Combined Groups

according to these hypotheses. Whether one emphasizes modeling the original intention of simple summation of responses, and then checking if the data collected satisfy the intention through a check on the model, or whether one emphasizes the modeling of the data collected, governs whether one chooses the Rasch model or the model of equation 6.4 for data of the ENS kind.

Effects of sample size. It was indicated earlier that the degree of misfit according to the χ^2 statistic is directly related to the sample size. This effect is reflected when the χ^2 is calculated for the males and females separately. Thus, while $\chi^2_L = 132.25$ on 20 df for the whole group, it has the smaller values of 63.77 and 90.02 on 20 df for males and females, respectively. These results do not necessarily imply that the data from either sex fit better, although they may. We have already seen that there are systematic differences between the sexes, therefore, the differences in the χ^2 are due, most likely, in part to sex differences and in part to differences in sample size.

Person Fit (Profiles)

While we have stressed the simultaneous scaling of the item and person parameters, so far we have studied the fit only of the items. However, the misfit of items results from relatively inconsistent responses of some persons. Thus the analysis of fit can also be made at the person level. Such analyses, conducted at a *microlevel* of analysis, have been called "person-fit," in parallel to "item-fit," but they can also be envisaged as analyses of profiles of persons.

To orient to person fit, recall that the total score of a person (r_n) is sufficient for the estimate of β_n. Therefore the same estimate is obtained for a total score, for a particular set of items, irrespective of the pattern of responses. At first glance this may seem surprising: It might be argued

TABLE 6.5
Relative Odds of Endorsement Between Items 1 and 3
Classified by Sex

	Items		Sex		
	1	3	M	F	
					$\chi^2 = 13.74$
Total	0	1	39	18	df = 1
Responses	1	0	343	452	$p < 0.05$
Odds ratio			0.114	0.040	

that if a person endorses a more affective item than another person in the ENS, then that person should be characterized as more neurotic. According to the same argument, in achievement testing a person who answers a difficult item correctly, rather than any easy one, should have a greater ability estimate.

Studying response patterns. There are two counters to that argument, one informal and one formal. Informally, suppose persons A and B obtain the same total score on the same items; then if person A has answered a more difficult item correctly and person B has answered it incorrectly, person A must have answered an easier item incorrectly that person B has answered correctly. It might be argued that person A should be penalized as much for answering an easy item incorrectly as he or she is rewarded for answering the difficult one correctly. Answering an easy item incorrectly may imply that the person is not that able. An analogous case can be made for a scale composed of affective items, such as the ENS. Alternatively, the unexpected responses may need clinical investigation. We turn to that perspective shortly.

Formally, response patterns in which items with large scale values receive a score of 1 and those with a low value receive scores of 0 are relatively unlikely in scales intended to be cumulative. As seen already, the probability of each pattern, given the total score, can be calculated, and if a pattern is extremely unlikely, it may be considered that the person has not been measured properly. *Thus, while the response pattern of a person is irrelevant to the estimate of location, it is crucial to the study of fit.* And the study of the pattern of responses may be termed a *profile analysis*. From such an analysis it may be deemed necessary for the person to respond to other items or to be interviewed for a clinical assessment.

Table 6.6 shows some response patterns in the ENS and the probability of their occurrence, given the total scores. Clearly, with items ordered according to their affective values, the patterns with 0s on the left have a lower probability of occurrence than those with 0s on the right. As indicated earlier, for a given score, the Guttman pattern has the highest probability.

Statistically one expects a small number of responses that are counter-intuitive; therefore, it might be considered inappropriate to reconsider each individual with such a response pattern. However, one may shift the orientation of the analysis from one with a statistical population in mind to one with the individual in mind. Then it becomes pertinent to ask why this individual, among many individuals, responded in an unusual way.

One further point should be made to consolidate this aspect of person measurement. *If two different sets of items, located on the same scale, are used, then the same score on the two sets will give different location estimates.* This feature is exploited in tailored achievement testing where more able persons are tested with more difficult items than are the less able. For example, suppose there are two sets of six items with the scale values as shown in Table 6.7. The entire 12 items have an origin of 0.0, and they have been divided into a set of the most difficult and a set of the least difficult items. It is evident from Table 6.7 that a score on the more difficult set corresponds to a greater location than does the same score on the easier set. Such transformations are very important in the study of intellectual growth and development (Fischer, 1976).

Response patterns and large item sets. The above approach to the study of response patterns is cumbersome when there are many items, as in many attitude and achievement tests in which 20 to 100 items or more are common. In an alternate approach, patterns are characterized by a summary of the differences between the observed and expected responses across items (Wright and Stone, 1979; Masters, 1982; Andrich, 1986).

Let

$$z_{ni} = (x_{ni} - E[X_{ni}])/\sqrt{V[X_{ni}]} = (x_{ni} - \pi_{ni})/\sqrt{\pi_{ni}(1 - \pi_{ni})}$$

be the standardized difference (residual) between the observed and expected response of person n to item i. Then for the SLM, the two possible residuals, z_{ni0} and z_{ni1}, when $x_{ni} = 0$ and 1 respectively, simplify to

$$z_{ni0} = -\sqrt{\pi_{ni}(1 - \pi_{ni})}; \qquad z_{ni1} = \sqrt{(1 - \pi_{ni})/\pi_{ni}} \qquad [6.7]$$

TABLE 6.6
Some Response Patterns and Probabilities
for the ENS Example

Pattern $(X_{ni})^a$						Probability $\Pr\left\{(x_{ni}) \mid r_n\right\}$	r_n
Items							
(1	6	4	2	5	3)		
1	0	0	0	0	0^b	0.378	1
0	0	1	0	0	0	0.112	1
0	0	0	0	1	0	0.058	1
1	1	0	0	0	0^b	0.326	2
0	1	1	0	0	0	0.096	2
0	0	0	1	1	0	0.016	2
1	1	1	0	0	0^b	0.218	3
0	1	1	0	1	0	0.034	3
0	0	0	1	1	1	0.003	3
1	1	1	1	0	0^b	0.275	4
0	1	1	1	1	0	0.042	4
0	0	1	1	1	1	0.005	4
1	1	1	1	1	0^b	0.417	5
1	1	1	0	1	1	0.136	5
0	1	1	1	1	1	0.037	5

a. Items ordered according to increasing affective values.
b. The Guttman pattern.

These differences provide a locus and Figure 6.5 shows this locus with respect to the location estimate of the person. Both of these patterns were observed in the data from the linking of the RPM reported in the previous chapter. Figure 6.5a shows the residuals for a person with a very systematic pattern—in fact, a Guttman pattern—while Figure 6.5b shows the residuals for a very erratic pattern. In the first case, the residuals are small in magnitude, while in the second case they are both large and small in magnitude. As in the case of deviations about the mean, the sum of these residuals is always 0. Therefore, to form an index of the general dispersion of the residuals, they may be squared and summed. Clearly, in a Guttman pattern, this sum of squared residuals is small, while in an erratic pattern it is large. (In Figure 6.5a, $\Sigma_i z_{ni}^2 = 5.12$ and in Figure 6.5b, $\Sigma_i z_{ni}^2 = 57.57$.) In fact, the sum of the squared residuals will be a minimum for the Guttman pattern and the maximum for the exact opposite.

TABLE 6.7
Person Location Estimates for Sets of Items
with Different Scale Values

Items	Scale Values Set 1	Scale Values Set 2	Raw Score	Location (β_r) and Standard Error (σ_r) Set 1		Set 2	
1	−2.50	0.00	0	−		−	
2	−2.00	0.50	1	−3.14	(1.16)	−0.60	(1.16)
3	−1.50	1.60	2	−2.08	(0.94)	0.44	(0.94)
4	−1.00	1.50	3	−1.26	(0.89)	1.26	(0.89)
5	−0.50	2.00	4	−0.44	(0.94)	2.08	(0.94)
6	0.00	2.50	5	0.60	(1.16)	3.14	(1.16)
			6	−		−	

The more usual criterion with which $\Sigma_i z_{ni}^2$ is compared is its expected value, which, if there were no estimation of parameters from the data, would be L, the number of items: With estimation it is approximately $L - 1$. The variance of $\Sigma_i z_{ni}^2$ is a function of $(\beta_n - \delta_i)$. Therefore one transformation of $\Sigma_i z_{ni}^2$ is simply to form its standardized residual giving

$$Y_n = [\sum_i z_{ni}^2 - (L - 1)] / \sqrt{V[\sum_i z_{ni}^2]}$$

Then a value of Y_n which is negative and large in magnitude implies a Guttman pattern and a positive value large in magnitude implies an erratic pattern, while a value close to 0.0 implies a typical pattern. (In Figure 6.5a, $Y_n = -0.98$ and in Figure 6.5b, $Y_n = 4.28$.) The study of the degree of dispersion of a set of responses about their expected values can be seen readily as the study of the profile or shape of the responses, following the identification of their location. The values of Y_n are shown in Table 5.4 for a select number of cases.

There are two consequences that follow from $V[\Sigma_i z_{ni}^2]$ being a function of $(\beta_n - \delta_i)$ that need to be appreciated. First is that when $\beta_n = \delta_i$, $V[z_{ni}^2] = 0$; therefore, there is no power in the test of fit with that item. But this is as it should be: The greater the difference between a person's ability and an item's difficulty, the less likely an unexpected response and therefore the more meaningful when it occurs.

Second, when all items have the same difficulty, there is no distinction among the probabilities of the response patterns—the probabilities are the same—and again there is no power in this test of fit. Therefore, it

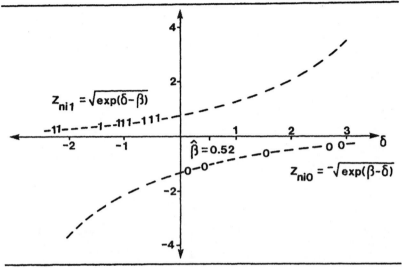

Figure 6.5a: Locus of Residuals for a Guttman Pattern. $Y_n = -0.98$

is necessary that the items cover a range of difficulty for the test of fit to be meaningful; but without items covering a range, no continuum is defined, only a point. Thus the power of the test of fit depends on the location of the person with respect to the scale values of the items and with respect to their spread. These statistics expose again the need to remain aware that a variable is being constructed and that the fit tests are concerned with the quality of its construction and its operation, in general and in specific cases. Here one finds the usual trade-off between reliability and validity: When the items are close to a person then one has precise measurement, but one has little power in checking the quality of the measurement, and vice versa. This brief analysis also reinforces the distinction between scale construction and person measurement. There is need for further research on the statistics for the study of profiles of persons, but at this stage the statistic Y_n can be used safely to order persons according to the consistency of their responses for items that have a spread of difficulties.

Because $\Sigma_i z_{ni}^2$ is skewed, various adjustments have been made to Y_n in order to make it more symmetric and to approximate a normal distribution (Wright and Stone, 1979; Andrich, 1980; Wright and Masters, 1982). Such adjustments make it easier to make fine points of interpretation, although Y_n itself is adequate to identify unusual patterns that

82

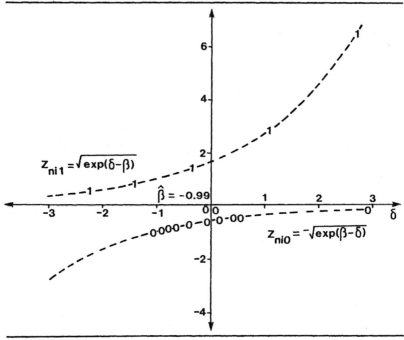

Figure 6.5b: Locus of Residuals for an Erratic Pattern. $Y_n = 4.28$

then can be studied individually. In achievement testing, a high value for this statistic may imply that very difficult items have been responded to correctly but unexpectedly. If that is the case, then it might imply guessing. Alternatively, it might imply specific knowledge resulting from special training, interests, or experience. Wright and Stone (1979) discuss the management of unusual response patterns. Sometimes a Guttman pattern, or one close to it, may also give cause for concern. Among many possibilities is that the person has failed to finish the test (a second factor of speed is contaminating the unidimensionality), or that some error has occurred in the coding, either by the respondent or by the coders (even when it is a machine that does the coding).

We have emphasized the summing of z_{ni}^2 over items to give a statistic indexing the volatility of the response profile for the person. However, these squared residuals may be summed over items with parallel interpretations: A very small value implies an item with a Guttman-like pattern and a very large value implies an erratic pattern, when the persons are ordered by their total scores. Thus the former indicates an item that, according to traditional criteria, has a high discrimination, while the latter indicates an item that has a low discrimination. Thus another approach to the study of item-fit is available. It is the one used most commonly by Wright and Stone (1979) and Wright and Masters (1982).

One final point should be made. This is that any misfit of persons is not independent of the misfit of items, and the other way around. Both are functions of the same data and their accord with the model. The distinction between the two, and a study of both, can help identify their prime sources. Thus all items could fit quite well, but some might appear to be marginal because of the responses of a few people, and vice versa. Therefore, as with the emphasis on the simultaneous scaling of person and item parameters, it is important to emphasize the need to study the simultaneous fit of items and persons.

Relationships to traditional test theory. It is appropriate to consider some relationships between traditional test theory (TTT) and the SLM in this section on fit because it is here that important similarities and differences between them are found. The SLM can be seen as refining and clarifying TTT and a case along these lines will be made here. Consequently, the connections made between TTT and the SLM are brief and selective and highlight only a few of the vast array of results of TTT (Gulliksen, 1950; Lord and Novick, 1968).

First, as in the SLM, in TTT the total unweighted score $r_n = \Sigma_i x_{ni}$ characterizes the person fully. However, in the SLM this statistic arises as a consequence of a model specified at the item level, while in TTT it is simply postulated as the appropriate test statistic to characterize a person. Second, again as in the SLM, the statistic r_n is used to estimate an unknown location parameter for a person. In TTT, this parameter is generally termed the true score τ_n, and it is postulated to be linearly related to r_n according to $r_n = \tau_n + \epsilon_n$ in which ϵ_n is a normally distributed random error. Effectively, in TTT the observed score r_n is regressed linearly on the latent trait: In the SLM it is regressed nonlinearly.

The scale values of the items are defined differently in the two approaches. In TTT, the proportions of correct responses in a group of persons, $p_i = \Sigma_i x_{ni}/N = s_i/N$, are used to indicate the items' easinesses (the inverse of difficulty) and therefore these are relative to the distribution of locations of the class of persons responding. As we have seen, in the SLM the scale values are defined relative to each other and therefore are independent of the distribution of locations of the persons.

Nevertheless, as shown in Chapter 5 and above, the relationship between the locations (β_n) and difficulties (δ_i) is relevant to the application of tests according to the SLM. Furthermore, from both TTT and the SLM (and commonsense) items should neither be too difficult nor too easy for a person. In TTT, the focus is on the sample, and it is considered desirable to have as many items as possible that have success rate of around 50%; in the SLM, the focus is on the individual and the difficulty value that gives a person a probability of success of 0.5 is understood to be the most informative about the person's location. Here a contrast emerges between TTT and the SLM. In the latter, the lack of homogeneity of the standard error of measurement is both clear and plausible. In the former it is taken to be homogeneous, although no one takes this property of the theory seriously except with very long tests that are used with samples where the floor and ceiling effects do not operate.

An important index in TTT is the internal consistency reliability ρ_{rr}, which may be defined in various ways through all may be reduced to some form such as

$$\rho_{rr} = \{V[R] - V[E]\}/V[R] \qquad [6.8]$$

where R is the random variable of raw scores across persons (usually denoted by X but denoted here by R for consistency with our use of r for the observed raw total score) and V[E] is the error variance. One popular estimate of ρ_{rr} is given by the Kuder-Richardson formula (KR.20):

$$KR.20 = (L/L - 1)\{V[R] - \Sigma_i p_i(1 - p_i)\}/V[R] \qquad [6.9]$$

Now let the SLM estimate $\hat{\beta}_n$ be resolved according to $\hat{\beta}_n = \beta_n + \epsilon_n$ where ϵ_n is the standard error of measurement. Then a reliability index, termed by Andrich and Douglas (1977) to be an index of person separation and denoted by r_β, and analogous to the KR.20 index, can be constructed. Specifically,

$$r_\beta = \{V[\hat{\beta}] - V[e]\}/V[\hat{\beta}] \qquad [6.10]$$

where $V[\hat{\beta}]$ is estimated by $\Sigma_n(\hat{\beta}_n - \bar{\hat{\beta}}_n)^2/(N-1)$ and $V[e] = \Sigma_n \dot{\sigma}_n^2/N$ is the average error variance across persons. But for the factor $(L/L - 1)$, the KR.20 and the values r_β values are virtually identical (Andrich, 1982). In the ENS data they have the respective values of 0.36 and 0.32, as shown in Table 6.8.

TABLE 6.8
Point Biserial Correlations Between
Responses to Each Item and the Total Score,
and Reliability Indices

Item	Point Biserial	
1	0.47	
2	0.67	(TTT) KR.20 = 0.36
3	0.48	
4	0.47	(SLM) r_β = 0.32
5	0.40	
6	0.43	

Although the values of KR.20 and r_β are virtually identical, the construction of r_β from the perspective of the SLM makes it clear that it is a property of the estimates of β for a sample provided by a test or questionnaire, and not a property of the test.

Two further points on the relationship between TTT and the SLM. First, in both, the operating quality or fit of the item is checked by noting how persons with varying total scores respond to the item. We have seen how this is done with the SLM. In TTT, the correlation between responses to items and the total score across persons is obtained as an index of the discrimination of the item. These correlations are routinely taken to indicate the quality of the items. Being simply a coefficient expressing a linear relationship between a total score and an item score, it provides a less refined indication of the variation of the responses to the item as a function of the total score than does the SLM analysis. Table 6.8 shows these correlations for the ENS data.

Finally, in Table 6.8, item 2 shows the highest discrimination and item 5 shows the lowest: This, of course, is the same conclusion drawn from the graphical SLM analysis. However, different general conclusions are made from these results when one takes the SLM perspective rather than the TTT perspective. With TTT, it is generally assumed that the greater the discrimination the better, because this increases the reliability, even though it is known from the attenuation paradox literature of TTT (Loevinger, 1954), that a reliability can be too high—that is, increase in reliability beyond a certain point leads to a decrease in validity. But an item helps increase the reliability when it has a high discrimination, that is, when it correlates very highly with other items. From the SLM perspective, it is noted immediately when an item discriminates "too highly." This is another manifestation of the explicit recognition that the total score of a test is transformed simultaneously with the item difficulties. Thus the SLM formalizes the tension between reliability and validity which is dealt with only informally in TTT: When an item or items discriminate too highly relative to the other items, then it or they begin contributing redundant information relative to the other items and begin to increase the reliability at the expense of validity.

Conclusion

This chapter considered a variety of procedures for checking the accord between the SLM and the data. Two important points emerged from applying these procedures. First, different tests of fit can be constructed to test different emphases in the way the responses may violate the model, and these different tests can have different power in detecting violations. There is nothing new here from the point of using fit statistics with models. Second, and what is perhaps new, is that with the application of the Rasch model, the boundaries between the use of statistical analyses and substantive analyses is more clear than with the application of other models: When the Rasch model is intended to hold because of its special measurement properties, failure of the data to conform to the model implies further work on the substantive problem of scale construction, not on the identification of a more complex model that might account for the data. Finally, the chapter related the principles for checking the fit of the data to the SLM with traditional test theory and, in particular, with the traditional reliability and discrimination indices.

Appendix A: Computation of π_{ri} from the Conditional Approach

π_{ri} is the probability that a person with a total score of r obtains a score of 1 on item i. Summing across equation 4.8 for $x_{ni} = 1$, given r, gives

$$p_{ri} = \sum_{((x_{ni})\mid r)} \Pr\{x_{ni} = 1; (\delta_i)\mid r\}$$

$$= \sum_{((x_{ni})\mid r)} \Pr\{(x_{ni}); (\delta_i)\mid r, x_{ni} = 1\} \qquad [A.1]$$

For the case of three items, for example

$$\pi_{21} = \Pr\{(1, 1, 0)\mid r = 2\} + \Pr\{(1, 0, 1)\mid r = 2\}$$

$$= [\exp(-\delta_1 - \delta_2) + \exp(-\delta_1 - \delta_3)]/\gamma_2$$

$$= \exp(-\delta_1)[\exp(-\delta_2) + \exp(-\delta_3)]/\gamma_2$$

$$= \exp(-\delta_1)\,\gamma_{1,1}/\gamma_2$$

In general

$$\pi_{ri} = \exp(-\delta_i)\,\gamma_{r-1,i}/\gamma_r \qquad [A.2]$$

in which $\gamma_{r-1,i}$ is the elementary symmetric function of order r with item i eliminated.

Appendix B: Properties of the Response Residual

$$z_{ni} = (x_{ni} - E[X_{ni}])/\sqrt{V[X_{ni}]} = (x_{ni} - \pi_{ni})/\sqrt{\pi_{ni}(1 - \pi_{ni})} \qquad [B.1]$$

$$\therefore z_{ni0} = (0 - \pi_{ni})/\sqrt{\pi_{ni}(1 - \pi_{ni})} = -\sqrt{\pi_{ni}/(1 - \pi_{ni})},$$

$$z_{ni1} = (1 - \pi_{ni})/\sqrt{\pi_{ni}(1 - \pi_{ni})} = \sqrt{(1 - \pi_{ni})/\pi_{ni}}$$

However, $\pi_{ni} = \exp(\beta_n - \delta_i)/(1 + \exp(\beta_n - \delta_i)) = \exp(\gamma_{ni})/\gamma_{ni}$

$$\therefore \; z_{ni0}^2 = \exp(\lambda_{ni}), \quad z_{ni1}^2 = \exp(-\lambda_{ni}) \qquad [B.2]$$

With no estimation of parameters,

$$E[Z_{ni}^2] = \sum_x \pi_{nix} \, Z_{nix}^2$$

$$= \exp(\lambda_{ni}) \, 1/\gamma_{ni} + \exp(-\lambda_{ni}) \exp(\lambda_{ni})/\gamma_{ni}$$

$$= \pi_{ni} + (1 - \pi_{ni}) = 1$$

$$\therefore \; E[\sum_i Z_{ni}^2] = \sum_i E[Z_{ni}^2] = L \qquad [B.3]$$

Analogously,

$$V[Z_{ni}^2] = E[Z_{ni}^4] - E^2[Z_{ni}]$$

$$= \exp\{2(\lambda_{ni})\} \, 1/\gamma_{ni} + \exp\{2(-\lambda_{ni})\} \exp(\lambda_{ni})/\gamma_{ni} - 1$$

which on simplification reduces to

$$V[Z_{ni}^2] = [\exp(-\lambda_{ni}) - \exp\lambda_{ni})] \, [1 - \exp(\lambda_{ni})]/[1 + \exp(\lambda_{ni})] \qquad [B.4]$$

Clearly, when $\lambda_{ni} = 0$, that is, when $\beta_n = \delta_i$, $V[Z_{ni}^2] = 0$ and, therefore,

$$V[\sum_i Z_{ni}^2] = 0.$$

It can also be shown that when $\delta_i = \delta$ for all i, then also

$$V[\sum_i Z_{ni}^2] = 0.$$

In these two extreme cases, there is no power in the test of fit. The items must be spread for evidence of a breakdown in the measurement on a continuum to be exposed. With all items of the same scale value there is no continuum, only a point.

As $\delta_i \lll \beta_n$, $V[Z_{ni}^2] \rightarrow \exp(\lambda_{ni})$; as $\beta_n \lll \delta_i$, $V[Z_{ni}^2] \rightarrow \exp(-\lambda_{ni})$.

NOTES

1. Andersen (1972) has shown that the conditional estimates are consistent in that as the number of persons increases, so the estimates converge on the values of the items.

2. A program that carries out the estimation and tests of fit in the above form is available from the author.

REFERENCES

ACER (1958) and RAVEN, J. C. et al. (1938) "Standard progressive matrices." Victoria: Australian Council for Educational Research.

ALLERUP, P. and G. SORBER (1977) The Rasch Model for Questionnaires. Copenhagen: Danish Institute for Educational Research.

ANDERSEN, E. B. (1972) "The numerical solution of a set of conditional estimation equations." Journal of the Royal Statistical Society 34 (Series B): 42-54.

ANDERSEN, E. B. (1973a) "A goodness of fit test for the Rasch Model." Psychometrika 38: 123-140.

ANDERSEN, E. B. (1973b) "Conditional inference for multiple choice questionnaires." British Journal of Mathematical and Statistical Psychology 26: 31-44.

ANDERSEN, E. B. (1977) "Sufficient statistics and latent trait models." Psychometrika 42: 69-81.

ANDERSEN, E. B. (1980) Discrete Statistical Models with Social Science Applications. Amsterdam: North Holland.

ANDRICH, D. (1978) "Relationships between the Thurstone and Rasch approaches to item scaling." Applied Psychological Measurement 3: 446-460.

ANDRICH, D. (1982) "An index of person separation in latent trait theory, the traditional KR.20 index, and the Guttman Scale response pattern." Educational Research and Perspectives 9: 95-104.

ANDRICH, D. (1985) "An elaboration of Guttman Scaling with Rasch Models for measurement," pp. 33-80 in N. Brandon-Tuma (ed.) Sociological Methodology, 1985. San Francisco: Jossey-Bass.

ANDRICH, D. (1986) "Intellectual development of pre-adolescent and adolescent children from a psychometric perspective." International Conference on Longitudinal Methodology, Budapest, Hungary, September.

ANDRICH, G. and G. A. DOUGLAS (1977) "Reliability: distinctions between item consistency and subject separation with the simple logistic model." Presented at the annual meeting of the American Educational Research Association, New York.

ANDRICH, D. and P. KLINE (1981) "Within and among population item fit with the simple logistic model." Educational and Psychological Measurement 41: 35-48.

BARNES, B. (1982) T. S. Kuhn and Social Science. London: Macmillan.

BIRNBAUM, A. (1968) "Some latent trait models and their use in inferring an examinee's ability," pp. 397-549 in F. Lord and M. Novick (eds.) Statistical Theories of Mental Test Scores, 1968. Reading, MA: Addison-Wesley.

BISHOP, Y. M., S. E. FEINBERG, and P. W. HOLLAND (1975) Discrete Multivariate Analysis: Theory and Practice. Cambridge: MIT Press.

BRADLEY, R. A. and M. E. TERRY (1952) "Rank analysis of incomplete block designs, I: The method of paired comparisons." Biometrika 39: 324-345.

CHOPPIN, B. (1968) "An item bank using sample-free calibration." Nature 219: 870-872.
CHOPPIN, B. (1983) A Fully Conditional Estimation Procedure for Rasch Model Parameters, Report No. 196. Los Angeles: University of California, Graduate School of Education Center for the Study of Evaluation.
COOMBS, C. H. (1964) A Theory of Data. New York: John Wiley.
DUNCAN, O. D. (1984) Notes on Social Measurement. New York: Russell Sage Foundation.
EDWARDS, A. L. and L. L. THURSTONE (1952) "An internal consistency check for scale values determined by the method of successive integers." Psychometrika 17: 169-180.
ELLIS, B. (1966) Basic Concepts in Measurement. Cambridge: Cambridge University Press.
EYSENCK, W. J. (1958) "A short questionnaire for the measurement of two dimensions of personality." Journal of Applied Psychology 47: 14-17.
EYSENCK, H. J. and S.B.G. EYSENCK (1964) Manual of the Eysenck Personality Inventory. London: University of London Press.
FISHER, G. (1981) "On the existence and uniqueness of maximum-likelihood estimates in the Rasch model." Psychometrika 46: 59-77.
FISHER, G. H. and H. SPADA (1973) Die Psychometrischen Grundlagen des Rorschachtests und der Holtzman Inkblot Technique. Vienna: Hans Huber.
GULLIKSEN, H. (1950) Theory of Mental Tests. New York: John Wiley.
GUSTAFSSON, J.-E. (1977) The Rasch Model for Dichotomous Items: Theory, Applications and a Computer Program, Report No. 63. Goteborg: University of Goteborg, Institute of Education.
GUSTAFSSON, J.-E. (1980a) "A solution of the conditional estimation problem for long tests in the Rasch model for dichotomous items." Educational and Psychological Measurement 40: 377-385.
GUSTAFSSON, J.-E. (1980b) "Testing and obtaining fit of data to the Rasch Model." British Journal of Mathematics and Statistical Psychology, 33: 205-233.
GUTTMAN, L. (1950) "The basis for scalogram analysis," pp. 60-90 in S. A. Stouffer (ed.) Measurement and Prediction, 1950. New York: John Wiley.
GUTTMAN, L. (1954) "The principal component of scalable attitudes," pp. 216-257 in P. F. Lazarsfield (ed.) Mathematical Thinking in the Social Sciences, 1954. New York: Free Press.
HABERMAN, S. J. (1977) "Maximum likelihood estimates in exponential response models." Annals of Statistics 5: 815-841.
HAMBLETON, R. K. [ed.] (1983) Applications of Item Response Theory. Vancouver: Educational Research Institute of British Columbia.
HUGHES, J. (1980) The Philosophy of Social Research. London: Longman.
HULIN, C. L., F. DRASGOW, and C. K. PARSONS (1983) Item Response Theory. Homewood, IL: Dow Jones-Irwin.
KELDERMAN, H. (1984) "Loglinear Rasch Model tests." Psychometrika 49: 222-245.
KNOKE, D. and P. J. BURKE (1980) Log-linear Models. Newbury Park, CA: Sage.
KRANTZ, D. H., R. D. LUCE, P. SUPPES, and A. TVERSKY (1971) Foundations of Measurement, Vol. 1. New York: Academic Press.
KRUSKAL, J. B. and M. WISH (1978) Multidimensional Scaling. Newbury Park, CA: Sage.

KUHN, T. S. (1961) "The function of measurement in modern physical science." ISIS 52 (Part 2): 161-193.
KUHN, T. S. (1970) The Structure of Scientific Revolutions. Chicago: University of Chicago Press.
LOEVINGER, J. (1954) "The attenuation paradox in test theory." Psychological Bulletin 51: 493-504.
LUCE, R. D. (1959) Individual Choice Behavior. New York: John Wiley.
LUCE, R. D. and J. W. TUKEY (1964) "Simultaneous conjoint measurement: new type of fundamental measurement." Journal of Mathematical Psychology 1: 1-27.
MASTERS, G. N. (1982) "A Rasch Model for partial credit scoring." Psychometrika 47: 149-174.
McIVER, J. P. and E. G. CARMINES (1981) Unidimensional Scaling. Newbury Park, CA: Sage.
MEAD, R. J. (1976) The Assessment of Fit of Data to the Rasch Model Through Analysis of Residuals. Ph.D. dissertation, University of Chicago.
MILLER, G. A. (1962) Psychology: The Science of Mental Life. Middlesex: Pelican.
MOLENAAR, I. W. (1983) "Some improved diagnostics for failure of the Rasch Model." Psychometrika 48: 49-72.
PERLINE, R., B. D. WRIGHT, and H. WAINER (1979) "The Rasch Model as additive conjoint measurement." Applied Psychological Measurement 3: 237-256.
RAMSAY, J. O. (1975) "Review of foundations of measurement, Vol. I," by D. H. Krantz et al. Psychometrika 40: 257-262.
RASCH, G. (1960/1980) Probabilistic Models for Some Intelligence and Attainment Tests. Copenhagen: Danish Institute for Educational Research, 1960. (Expanded edition, Chicago: The University of Chicago Press, 1980.)
RASCH, G. (1961) "On general laws and the meaning of measurement in psychology," pp. 321-334 in Proceedings of the Fourth Berkeley Symposium on Mathematical Statistics and Probability, IV. Berkeley: University of California Press.
RASCH, G. (1966) "An item analysis which takes individual differences into account." British Journal of Mathematical and Statistical Psychology 19: 49-57.
RASCH, G. (1968) "A mathematical theory of objectivity and its consequences for model contribution." European Meeting on Statistics, Econometrics, and Management Science, Amsterdam.
RASCH, G. (1977) "On specific objectivity: an attempt at formalising the request for generality and validity of scientific statements." Danish Yearbook of Philosophy 14: 58-94.
ROBERTS, F. S. (1979) Measurement Theory. Reading, MA: Addison-Wesley.
ROSKAM, E. E. and P.G.W. JANSEN (1984) "A new derivation of the Rasch Model," pp. 293-307 in E. Degreef and J. Van Buggenhaut (eds.) Trends in Mathematical Psychology, 1984. New York: Elsevier.
STEVENS, S. S. (1946) "On the theory of scales of measurement." Science 103: 677-680. (Reprinted in Readings in Statistics, 1970, A. Haber et al., eds., Reading, MA: Addison-Wesley.)
THURSTONE, L. L. (1926) "The scoring of individual performance." Journal of Educational Psychology 17: 446-457.
THURSTONE, L. L. (1927a) "A law of comparative judgement." Psychological Review 34: 278-286.

94

THURSTONE, L. L. (1927b) "The method of paired comparisons for social values." Journal of Abnormal and Social Psychology 21: 384-400.
THURSTONE, L. L. (1927c) "Psychophysical analyses." American Journal of Psychology 38: 368-389.
THURSTONE, L. L. (1959) The Measurement of Values. Chicago: University of Chicago Press.
VAN den WOLLENBERG, A. L. (1982) "Two new statistics for the Rasch Model." Psychometrika 47: 123-140.
WEBB, E. J., D. T. CAMPBELL, R. D. SCHWARTZ, and L. SECHREST (1969) Unobtrusive Measures. Chicago: Rand McNally.
WRIGHT, B. D. (1968) "Sample-free test calibration and person measurement," pp. 85-101 in Proceedings of the 1967 Invitational Conference on Testing Problems. Princeton, NJ: Educational Testing Service.
WRIGHT, B. D. (1977) "Misunderstanding the Rasch Model." Journal of Educational Measurement 14: 219-225.
WRIGHT, B. D. (1984) "Despair and hope for educational measurement." Contemporary Education Review 3: 281-288.
WRIGHT, B. D. and G. A. DOUGLAS (1977) "Best procedures for sample-free item analysis." Applied Psychological Measurement 1: 281-294.
WRIGHT, B. D. and G. A. DOUGLAS (1986) "The two-category model for objective measurement," Research Memorandum No. 34. Chicago: University of Chicago, Department of Education, Statistical Laboratory.
WRIGHT, B. D. and G. N. MASTERS (1982) Rating Scale Analysis. Chicago: MESA Press.
WRIGHT, B. D. and R. J. MEAD (1976) "BICAL: calibrating items with the Rasch Model," Research Memorandum No. 23. Chicago: University of Chicago, Department of Education, Statistical Laboratory.
WRIGHT, B. D. and N. PANCHAPAKESAN (1969) "A procedure for sample-free item analysis." Educational and Psychological Measurement 29: 23-48.
WRIGHT, B. D. and M. H. STONE (1979) Best Test Design: Rasch Measurement. Chicago: MESA Press.

NOTES

DAVID ANDRICH is Professor of Education at Murdoch University in Western Australia. His current research is in the applications of fundamental measurement in the social sciences and in the relationships between qualitative and quantitative work to achieve such measurement.